May your marriage be ...

Husbands, love your wives . . .

Colossians 3:19

What
Wives
Expect of
Husbands

Brent A. Barlow

Deseret Book Company
Salt Lake City, Utah

© 1982 Deseret Book Company
All rights reserved
Printed in the United States of America
ISBN 0-87747-911-9
Library of Congress Catalog Card Number 82-70919

First printing March 1982

CONTENTS

PREFACE

Not long ago a young wife wrote to me: "I know my husband loves me, but he doesn't show it in the way I would like. It is so strange how a man can really love his wife and yet have absolutely no idea how to express it so she believes him."

The purpose of this book is to help husbands express love for their wives. It will also help wives make their important expectations known.

This book is obviously not an exhaustive report of "what is" in marriage. It is more of an indication of what "might be." And, if it helps make marital expectations known and then acted upon, the time and effort I have spent writing it will have been well spent.

After giving a lecture on love and marriage at Brigham Young University a few years ago, I was driving home and decided I wanted Susan, my wife, to know I loved her. I could buy her some flowers, tell her I love her, and then rush her off to some secluded restaurant. What else could a wife want?

I walked in the house with the flowers and announced my love. Susan looked a little suspicious. I told her that I wanted to do something to show my love and that I intended to take her out to dinner.

After a few moments, she said, "If you really want to show me you love me, go wash the dishes." I thought I was losing my hearing. "What was that again?" I asked. She repeated her request.

"You didn't hear me," I responded. "No, you didn't hear me," she said. Susan told me she had had a frustrating day. She was exhausted. She thanked me for the flowers and said she appreciated being told she was loved. But as far as going out for dinner, she would rather go another evening. "I haven't been able to get to the dishes yet," she said, "and there isn't anything you could do to show your love more than to wash the dishes."

I was overwhelmed! How could any wife prefer a little help around the house to going out for dinner?

Out to the kitchen I went and rolled up my shirt sleeves. As I was slopping around in the soap suds trying to be philosophical about the whole matter, it suddenly dawned on me that husbands and wives often perceive love differently. While my concept of love (as is usual with many men) often deals with doing something romantic, like going out to eat (I have since learned the common Pavlovian phenomenon of men associating good food and seclusion with romance), there are often many more effective ways to show a wife you love her.

I finished the dishes that evening and helped Susan with a few other tasks. She appreciated my help and was able to retire that evening at an earlier hour because of it. We didn't go out that evening, but I had learned a valuable lesson about love.

It is now evident to me that (1) most husbands love their wives, and (2) husbands often try to show their love in ways other than their wives would like them to.

Not long after this experience, I began writing a weekly newspaper column on marriage for the *Deseret News*. For one of the columns, I related my experience and asked wives to write to me and respond to two questions: (1) What had their husbands done to show their love that the wives appreciated most? and (2) What could their husbands do in the future to show their love that the wives would appreciate?

As my secretaries and I began reading the many responses, we found that certain statements appeared over and over. A profile emerged of what a loving husband would be like. (See Appendix B, "Profile of a Loving Husband.")

During winter semester 1981 at Brigham Young University, I taught a marriage seminar for husbands, wives, and engaged couples. I shared some of my findings and asked the students to respond to the two questions I had asked in the newspaper column. We compared their answers with those I received in the mail. The results were similar. From these numerous responses, we decided to pick twenty that appeared most frequently and test them for priority of importance.

In the marriage class, the women responded, and ten items appeared to have high priority. In the *Deseret News*, I mentioned the "Profile of a Loving Husband" and asked wives to write for the profile, pick the ten most important items, and rank them in order of importance. Nearly two hundred women wrote for the profile and later returned the questionnaire. I compared the responses to those of my students. The rankings were similar, suggesting consistency in what many wives wanted or expected in a husband. This later suggested the basic idea for this book.

You and your spouse might read this book individually or together. Then you may want to write your own profiles of a loving husband and wife.

Since expectations vary from person to person, no two people will make exactly the same profile. Also, expectations may differ at various stages of marriage. Therefore, a periodic review of expectations seems essential. One aid in such a review is "Measuring Your Marriage Potential" in Appendix C.

The importance of couples' learning to make changes in their marriages was noted by President Spencer W. Kimball: "We are concerned over the mounting number of divorces not only in our society, but in the Church. We are just as concerned with those whose families and marriages seem to be held together in 'quiet desperation.' "[1]

Dr. Sidney Jourard, marriage counselor and psychotherapist in Gainesville, Florida, said:

> I have been struck by the incredible lack of artistry and creativity in marriage partners. Either person may be imaginative in making money or decorating a house,

but when it comes to altering the design for their relationship, it is as if both imaginations had burnt out.

For years spouses go to sleep night after night, with
their relationship patterned one way, a way that perhaps satisfies neither—too close—too distant, boring
or suffocating—and on awakening the next morning
they reinvent their relationship in the same way.

There is nothing sacred to the wife about the way
she decorated her house; as soon as it begins to pall, she
shuffles things around until the new decor pleases her.
But the way she and her husband interact will often per-
sist for years unchallenged and unchanged, long after it
has ceased to engender delight, zest, or growth. [2]

A husband and wife must learn to make their own expectations known and make reasonable attempts to meet each other's realistic expectations. This book provides some thoughts
on how this may be done.

One final note. Some may be offended that a man (and husband) has written a book about the expectations of wives. I
have two defenses. First, I have spent several hundred hours
during the past ten years counseling and listening to numerous
wives and husbands. From these sessions, I have gained a few
insights and opinions. Second, I have recently reviewed several hundred questionnaires and read numerous letters written
by women. And from my listening and reading, I would like to
share with you what I have learned. You will have to draw your
own conclusions about my objectivity.

I appreciate the more than three hundred wives who responded to questionnaires or sent me letters about what they
expected of their husbands.

Thanks also to Don Woodward, editor of the "Today" sec-
tion of the Deseret News; Carma Wadley; and others on the
Deseret News staff who have made my column on marriage possible.

Special thanks to the secretarial staff of the Department of
Family Sciences at Brigham Young University, who not only
typed the original manuscript, but gave several insights on

husband-wife relationships as well. Assistance in proofreading was provided by the Faculty Support Center at the College of Family, Home, and Social Sciences at Brigham Young University.

The staff and editors at Deseret Book have been very helpful and supportive of this book since it was proposed. Particular thanks to Jack Lyon for his careful editing; Eleanor Knowles, editor and publishing manager; Ralph Reynolds, design director; and Lowell M. Durham, Jr., general manager; and to others who have assisted.

I appreciate the patience of my six children during the summer of 1981 while Dad wrote some book about marriage.

And to my wife, Susan, I give particular thanks not only for choosing the title for the book, but for other helpful comments and suggestions. Incidently, after reviewing the first draft of the book, she informed me I could have obtained most of the material from her personal journal and saved myself a lot of time and work.

1

COMMUNICATION

Although we speak our native language with reasonable clarity, the most difficult communication in the world is often between husband and wife. The inability of married couples to communicate is shown in the story of a middle-aged woman who walked into a lawyer's office to file for divorce. The lawyer asked her to sit down. He got out his pencil and yellow pad and asked the woman some questions.

"Do you have grounds?" he inquired.

"Yes," she replied, "about three-quarters of an acre."

The lawyer paused for a moment, then asked, "Do you have a grudge?"

"No," the woman quickly answered, "but we do have a lovely carport."

Again the lawyer paused. "Does he beat you up?"

"No, I get up before he does every morning."

Finally in exasperation the lawyer blurted out, "Lady, why do you want to divorce your husband?"

"Because," she explained, "that man cannot carry on an intelligent conversation."

One of the greatest consistencies of my survey is how frequently communication was mentioned as being important in marriage. As one wife wrote, "If you don't have communication, what does anything else matter?"

Of the twenty items in the "Profile of a Loving Husband," communication was consistently ranked the highest. (See Appendix B.) It was given first priority by thirty-eight percent of the wives; another twenty percent listed it as second most important. Nearly eighty percent listed communication as one of the top five characteristics of a loving husband, and it was listed almost ninety percent of the time as one of the top ten. Wives want, more than anything else the survey indicated, to have their husbands communicate with them.

Wives Comment

One wonders if husbands lose their ability to speak and listen when they cross the threshold as they return home each evening. When asked what their husbands could do to show their love, wives responded overwhelmingly in the area of communication. Consider the following comments by wives about husbands and communication:

"I wish my husband would listen and communicate with me, share joys, sorrows, fears, hopes, dreams, discouragements, weaknesses, and strengths. Nothing else could show caring as much as this. It is as much an act of faith as it is love. I wish he would involve me in his prime time and make me feel more important than work, customers, television, sports, hobbies, reading, or other people."

"One way my husband could show his love for me is in our communication. I get frustrated many times trying to talk to him about it. But he feels I am arguing and doesn't want to discuss it, or he doesn't respond the way I feel he should. All he would need to say is "I understand how you feel" or something like that."

"My husband could talk to me more and tell me his innermost feelings without me having to pry them out of him. He could also listen when I tell him something and comment after, even if what I had to say wasn't particularly interesting to him. Also, if he didn't want to listen, he could say so. That way I wouldn't have to continually repeat myself."

"In the future I would greatly appreciate more undivided attention when there are matters to discuss. The children, the chores, the phone, the television, work, and sleep make it difficult to get his undivided attention. I just wish my husband would find time to communicate with me."

"There is so much more to communication in a good marriage than talking about the weather and the children. There are so many times I wish my husband would both listen to my thoughts and feelings and express his to me. I would really feel we could be so much closer if we would talk to each other more about things that really matter. Otherwise he seems so distant and distracted."

"I would like my husband to open up and communicate more deeply with me. Many times his mind is so preoccupied with problems and concerns that I can hardly pry anything out of him. By having open communication where we share personal feelings, I feel we could become even closer than we are now."

"Something I would like my husband to do to show his love for me is to listen more attentively when I talk and respond to my questions with more than a simple *yes* or *no*. I need to know what he thinks about what I am saying."

Some husbands apparently prejudge what they think their wives are going to say:

"Mostly I wish my husband would pay more attention to my opinions and at least act as though they have servant of such things as drooped shoulders, a wrinkled brow, a slumped or tense body, all of which communicate feelings. If what we see conflicts with what we hear, we should report the contradiction to our spouse. To carefully observe, according to Dr. Kilgore, means to sense the mood of someone else's comments as well as hearing their words.

Verifying. To verify simply means to "check out" rather than assume. A productive part of communication is to clarify what is being communicated. Non-demanding questions such as "Is this what you mean?" or "Are you saying . . . ?" tend to move communication along. Dr. Kilgore believes that good communication moves on these clarifying responses. Being sure means having to say "I'm sorry" less.

Enhancing. To enhance means to intensify, magnify, or elevate the original message so that the sender recognizes that his or her comments have been understood. Husbands and wives who are good conversationalists are not only careful listeners but good responders as well. When one acknowledges what the other is saying, for example, a special bridge exists at that moment over which both can travel more freely.

If a husband and wife can remember LOVE and the four words it represents, listening, observing, verifying, and enhancing, they can improve communication in their marriage.

How Well Do You Communicate?

One of the most frequent statements I have heard over the years from troubled married couples is "We just can't communicate." And my response is "It is impossible *not* to communicate." What couples sometimes mean is they have a difficult time talking to each other or they are not talking at all. But silence is a high form of communication and is usually quite destructive. Mahatma Ghandi said, "Silence is for your enemies."

We often assume if we don't talk to someone, he will not know our feelings. But much of our communication, perhaps most, is nonverbal and needs to be clarified. The most effective form of communication, however, is speech.

6

Millard Bienvenu has devised a test to help determine how effective communication really is. For each of the following nineteen items respond with "usually," "sometimes," "seldom," or "never." Perhaps you and your spouse would like to take the test separately and then compare responses.

Measurement of Marital Communication[2]

	Usually	Sometimes	Seldom	Never
1. Does your spouse have a tendency to say things which would be better left unsaid?				
2. Do you find your spouse's tone of voice irritating?				
3. Does your spouse complain that you don't understand him/her?				
4. Does your spouse insult you when he/she gets angry with you?				
5. Do you fail to express disagreement with him/her because you're afraid he/she will get angry?				
6. Does it upset you a great deal when your spouse gets angry at you?				
7. Do you hesitate to discuss certain things with your spouse because you're afraid he/she might hurt your feelings?				
8. Do you find it difficult to express your true feelings to him/her?				
9. Is it easier to confide in a friend rather than your spouse?				
10. Does he/she seem to understand your feelings?				
11. Do you help your spouse to understand you by telling him/her how you think, feel, and believe?				
12. Does your spouse nag you?				
13. Do you feel he/she says one thing but really means another?				

	Usually	Sometimes	Seldom	Never
14. Do you pretend you're listening to your spouse when actually you are not really listening?				
15. Does he/she try to lift your spirits when you're depressed or discouraged?				
16. Does your spouse accuse you of not listening to what he/she says?				
17. Do you and your spouse engage in outside interests and activities together?				
18. Are you and your spouse able to disagree one with another without losing your tempers?				
19. Do you and your spouse ever sit down just to talk things over?				

According to Bienvenu, the items in "Measurement of Marital Communication" are listed in decreasing order of their importance in effective communication. That is, item 1 is more important than item 2, and item 2 is more important than 3. "Usually" is the best response to items 11, 15, 17, 18, and 19. "Never" would be the ideal response to the remaining items. [2]

By reviewing your responses together, you and your partner should better understand how you communicate. In addition, you might get some ideas to improve your communication.

The Memo Method

In their book *Marriage and the Memo Method*, [3] Dr. Paul Hauck and Dr. Edmund Kean state that if you do not know what your spouse is talking about, you won't understand what problems you face. Nor will you know how to deal with them. It is, therefore, extremely important for you to learn how to communicate your feelings and frustrations to your mate and for your mate to communicate his or hers to you.

But this is sometimes difficult. The best and perhaps easiest way to communicate is by speaking, as was pointed out earlier.

But husbands and wives often fail to talk about their thoughts and feelings because relatively few people want to listen. And when they do listen, they often ignore or do not believe what they are being told. In addition, as husbands and wives talk, they send numerous non-verbal messages that confuse or distort what they say.

To improve communication in marriage, Hauck and Kean outline the Memo Method, a way to write down one's feelings and thoughts and share them with a partner. Written notes made about grievances in the absence of the partner will likely have greater objectivity than an emotional, face-to-face confrontation.

The object of the Memo Method is to make husbands and wives think before they write down a thought, suggestion, or complaint. Nothing is more patient, the authors claim, than paper. Written and read in solitude, without interference of personalities, problems are stated much more objectively and less irritably.

Here are the three-steps of the Memo Method:

1. Write the word *Problem* in the upper-left hand corner of a sheet of paper. Then, as clearly and concisely as possible, state the problem. Try to limit it to one or two sentences.

2. Write the word *Causes* in the left-hand margin. Under this heading, list the ways both of you act or the things you say that contribute to the problem.

3. Write the word *Solutions* in the left-hand margin and list all the possibilities that you feel both you and your spouse can do to clear up the problem.

After you have completed these three steps, give your paper to your spouse. Allow him or her adequate time to read your thoughts when you are not present. Then he or she should follow the same three steps and respond in writing to your stated problem with alternative causes and solutions.

Now the stage is set to get together, and, through discussion, see if you agree on the problem. Both should accept responsibility for what he or she is or has been doing to contribute to the problem. Then you should agree on what might be done individually and as a couple to solve the problem.

If there is something in your marital relationship that you have found difficult to express verbally to your spouse, why not try the Memo Method. Just write down your thoughts and feelings and allow your spouse to read them before you talk. This should improve your ability to communicate.

Communicating Feelings

Not long ago, a husband told me the most difficult thing for him to do was to tell his wife about his good feelings for her. While many married couples have difficulty expressing their feelings about each other, some find they can do so with the Memo Method. After writing their thoughts and feelings on paper, most couples find the transition to verbal expression much easier.

William Miller and Larry Hof have begun an interesting program with the Marriage Council of Philadelphia. In their program, "My World of Feelings,"[4] they observe, "In a marital relationship, the ability of two individuals to be aware of the whole range of feelings, to express them appropriately, and to accept them in themselves and in each other, can pave the way for increased self-awareness and for stronger bonds of trust and deeper intimacy. It may make each partner more vulnerable, too. But, perhaps the potential for self-awareness and growth and for increased trust and intimacy is worth the risk!" (P. 98.)

Hof and Miller suggest a husband and wife individually write their responses to the following statements:

1. In our marriage, I am happiest when _____.
2. In our marriage, I am saddest when _____.
3. In our marriage, I am angriest when _____.
4. I feel most afraid when _____.
5. I feel loved when you _____.
6. I feel appreciated when you _____.
7. My greatest fear/concern for our marriage is _____.
8. The best thing about our marriage is _____.
9. What I like most about myself is _____.
10. What I dislike most about myself is _____.
11. What I like most about you is _____.

12. My greatest fear/concern for you is _____.

13. The feelings I have the most difficulty sharing with you are _____.

14. The feelings that I can share most easily with you are _____.

After completing the exercise, the husband and wife may exchange lists. Then they should discuss in further detail what each has written.

Hof and Miller conclude, "If my feelings are to serve me and help make sense in life, I must be aware of them and their heights and depths, and be able to express them appropriately in words and actions. In some way, I pay a great price when I refuse to let my feelings have an appropriate and natural place in my life." (P. 98.)

Shared Humor in Communication

It is obvious to most husbands and wives that many humorous incidents occur in marriage. Not long ago I got up late and reached in the bathroom cabinet for my aerosol deodorant. By mistake, I got my wife's hair spray. Susan got a good laugh out of it, but I failed to see much humor in the mix-up. In fact, I was miserable the rest of the day.

In their book *A Guide to Successful Marriage*,[5] Dr. Robert Harper and Dr. Albert Ellis note, "Perhaps nothing helps more than a sense of humor to establish or reestablish effective communication in marriage. It is easier, of course, to see humor in other people's marriage troubles than in one's own. It is also easier to find something funny about one's mate's predicaments than about one's own. For humor to facilitate marital communication, it must be shared by husband and wife." (P. 197.)

I recall another incident in our marriage a few years ago that verifies Harper and Ellis's observation about shared humor. Susan and I were fishing from the shore of a lake. She was on one side of a big bush and I was on the other. My wife's casting skills—how can I say it discreetly?—are better at some times than others. The fish were biting fairly well and I heard her wind up for a cast. There was a distinct whip of the rod and sud-

11

denly I felt a tug on my shirt collar. Susan called over that she had a snag. I called back "Yes, I know." Just then she began reeling in her line and pulling me into the bush. I finally yelled out that she had caught me with her indiscriminate casting. There was a short pause and then she began laughing. She thought it was so funny. As with the deodorant and hair spray mix-up, I didn't see the humor at all.

I tried to get the hook out of my collar, and just about the time I would have it out, she would give another tug on her line. I was getting more annoyed as the minutes went by. In fact, I was so irritated that I couldn't laugh with her at the incident. A couple of kids fishing down the bank thought the scene was rather entertaining and did my laughing for me.

After I got the hook out, I didn't feel like fishing anymore and it was getting late anyway. On the way home, I clammed up while Susan tried to talk to me about the matter. But at that moment, I just couldn't talk about it. Later on that evening, Susan related the event to the children, who laughed and laughed. By this time, I was able to agree that it was pretty funny. Earlier, however, I could not. Something has to be humorous to both partners before it will help their marriage.

Harper and Ellis ask, "Does this mean that married couples who want to learn and live happily together need to become rather nitwittish about difficulties? Does it take a third-rate comedian to succeed in modern marriage?" (P. 198.) They answer, "No, it takes acceptance, if not immediate resolution of differences. Since, however, anxiety is an omnipresent block to understanding and accepting and dealing rationally with differences between two intimate associates, and since humor is one of the best methods of reducing anxious blockings, shared humor in marriage is one of the better communication techniques." (P. 199.)

As Stephen Leacock noted, "humor may be defined as the kindly contemplation of the incongruities of life." By learning to laugh together at their marital inconsistencies, couples can improve marital communication and make contemporary living seem a little less hectic.

Dealing with Anger

One of the great inhibitors of effective communication in marriage is anger. When a husband or wife becomes angry, things are often said that cause further resentment. In addition, statements are sometimes made under the duress of anger that otherwise would not have been made. Elder Theodore M. Burton said, "Whenever you get red in the face, whenever you raise your voice, whenever you get 'hot under the collar,' or angry, rebellious, or negative in spirit, then know that the spirit of God is leaving you and the spirit of Satan is beginning to take over. (*Conference Report*, Oct. 1974, p. 77.)

In their book *How to Have a Happy Marriage*,[6] Dr. David and Vera Mace make some suggestions for dealing with anger in marriage. The Maces believe that anger is an involuntary, powerful feeling that takes hold of us when we are physically threatened or frustrated. Since few people in contemporary life are threatened for their day-to-day physical survival, most contemporary anger arises through frustration, particularly from unmet expectations.

In marriage, we often find ourselves in situations where expectations are high and frustrations can often occur. For normal people, being married may sometimes generate more anger than any other interpersonal situation.

How should a married couple deal with anger? First, the Maces advise, recognize that anger is a normal emotion that often develops spontaneously as a response to an outside stimulus. "A person who doesn't get angry," they state, "is not a normal human being."

Although we often have a difficult time not becoming angry, we are responsible for what we do about it. The Maces state: "People who say they have an 'uncontrollable' temper are deceiving themselves. They allow themselves to stamp and rage because at some time in their past temper tantrums enabled them to get what they wanted." (P. 112.)

Another common misunderstanding about anger is that by venting it, we get rid of it. The opposite is true. Venting anger sends a message to the body to continue its responses. Recent

13

studies have shown that those who vent their anger, tend, over time, to produce more and more anger. Venting anger vigorously usually leads to physical violence. And venting anger almost always gets your marriage partner angry, too. Then you require more and more anger to continue the fight.

David and Vera Mace suggest a three-step program to deal constructively with anger in marriage:

1. Agree to acknowledge your anger to each other as soon as you become aware of it. Acknowledging anger is not venting anger; it simply communicates to your partner the state of your emotions without accusation or blame.

2. Renounce together the right to vent anger on each other. Anger is damaging to a love relationship. There are better ways to deal with anger than venting it. Simply talking things through often helps.

3. Ask your spouse to help you deal with your anger.

The Maces conclude, "Only when you have brought anger completely under control in your marriage—and we mean by accepting and resolving it together, not suppressing it—does the way lay clear and open to a continuing growth in love and intimacy. (P. 115.)

We might be angry at times with each other in marriage. But we should learn to control what we do about it by dealing with our anger immediately, before it destroys communication.

The Backster Effect

The tone of voice is another important factor in communication. In our own marriage, Susan and I have never been able to agree on one thing: what constitutes yelling.

I claim yelling is what I do when I call the children home at night when they are down at the other end of the street. Susan says that yelling is talking in a critical and somewhat elevated tone. Her point is that how we talk to each other communicates as much if not more than what we say.

Susan recently took a course in elementary education called "Developing Positive Self-Concepts." She came home elated one night and said, "Here, read this." She handed me an article she had learned about in class. It was called "Plants Are Only Human."[7]

The article described an experience of Clive Backster, an eminent authority in the field of lie detection. One day, Mr. Backster was watering the plants in his office and was wondering how long it would take the water to get from the pot up to the top leaf. He decided to find out by using a polygraph to measure galvanic response.

Backster attached the electrodes to the plant leaf, and much to his surprise, there on the graph was a tracing that he, as a polygraph expert, had learned to recognize as an emotional reaction. Trying to find out what was going on, Backster threatened his plant by sticking a leaf into his cup of hot coffee. Nothing happened. Then he decided to do something more drastic. He muttered, "I'll burn the plant."

The needle on the chart immediately jumped upward!

The polygraph gave every indication that his plant had an emotional response when threatened. After conducting several other similar experiments, Clive Backster reported his findings in a paper published in the *International Journal of Parapsychology* describing what has become known as the "Backster Effect." Simply stated, plants supposedly respond to different emotional states of people. And they can apparently tell if you love them or hate them by the way you talk to them and act in their presence.

I was a little suspicious of the Backster Effect, so Susan suggested we try one of his experiments. We were supposed to get two similar plants and lavish one with praise and affection. We were to speak rudely to the other. The one getting the praise would supposedly flourish. The other would die. Better results were supposed to be obtained if both plants were in less-than-ideal soil and were watered less than usual.

But I was not too anxious to try the experiment. That you are talking to plants has a way of getting around the neighborhood. But I did agree to conduct an experiment with our garden. We divided the garden plants into two groups. Susan took the cucumbers, peppers, carrots, peas, and melons and intended to give them lots of praise and affection each day. I agreed to raise the tomatoes and corn. And what would I give them? Lots of water and fertilizer! And at the end of the summer we would see whose plants turned out the best.

The end of the summer did come. For some strange reason my corn was stunted and the tomatoes were only average. But I was still not convinced that her generous crop of cucumbers, peppers, carrots, peas, and melons was a result of praise and affection.

But it did give me something to think about. Maybe Susan was right. If talking harshly would affect plants, maybe it could also affect people. And if that's the case, I should have sneaked out late at night during our contest and spoken rudely to her plants. In the meantime, I have tried to watch my tone of voice when we discuss sensitive matters in our marriage.

Assuming and Asking

Let me point out two additional ways marital communication could be improved:

1. *Don't assume.* Husbands and wives frequently have lived together so long, they assume they automatically know what the other is feeling, thinking, or trying to say. This thought was implied in the popular film *Love Story*, which suggested that "Love means never having to say you're sorry." The implication is that your partner knows you so well you don't have to say anything. Most troubled husbands and wives have long assumed they understand what their mates mean by certain actions, or feel in certain situations, or intend by various words or gestures or tone of voice. Their negative assumptions about their mates' motives frequently produce the negative behavior that they have already assumed existed. By learning not to assume, we give our spouse the opportunity to be understood.

2. *Learn to ask.* Rather than assuming you know in advance what the other is feeling or is going to say, learn to ask your partner what he or she means, feels, thinks, or intends concerning even the most simple things in your marriage. You may find out you didn't really understand your partner as well as you thought.

A wife may ask her husband to say what he thinks she has said. If she says "Yes, that is right, that is what I actually meant," then and only then should her husband feel he understands.

This approach to improve marital communication may seem time-consuming and tedious. But if frequently practiced, it can be highly illuminating. William James wrote, "The most immutable barrier in nature is between one person's thoughts and another's." When husband and wife learn not to assume and to ask, part of the barrier will be removed.

A Communication Exercise

There are dozens of books and hundreds of articles written about communication. One such article was written by Paul Schuable and Clara Hill describing a communication exercise called "Training in Communication Skills."[8] I have slightly modified the exercise and found it to be useful.

Just for fun, it is recommended that husbands and wives tape record their conversations during this exercise and later critique what they have said. The exercise is done in three separate sessions.

Session one: Identifying sender and receiver. Schuable and Hill claim most of the problems in marital communication arise because we do not know who is sending the message and who is receiving it. Sometimes both partners are attempting to send and no one is receiving. According to this communication model, there can be only one sender and one receiver at a time.

So in session one we identify:

Partner A   *Partner B*

Sender ————————————————————▶ Receiver

After a couple decides who is going to be Sender and who is going to be Receiver, the conversation might go something like this: Paula, the new bride, would say to Richard, the new groom, "Richard, I have something to say to you." Richard could then reply, "All right, I am willing to receive it." Richard has no obligation at this point to do anything but hear what Paula has to say. She would then speak to Richard in a clear, concise manner. For instance, she might say, "I would appreciate it if you would occasionally help me wash the dishes after our evening meal."

Few couples want to do this exercise because it seems so obvious. But how often in marriage does one partner try to say something to a spouse who is oblivious to the fact that the other person is trying to say something? A beginning point in effective marital communication would be to identify one sender and one receiver at a time, since it is impossible for both to be senders simultaneously.

After Paula has sent her message to Richard (who makes no comment or elaborations), the two switch roles, and Richard then becomes Sender and Paula becomes Receiver. Richard then says something he would like her to know. For example, he might say, "I appreciated your typing my term paper for my class."

After being senders and receivers for several minutes, session one is completed.

Session two: Listening by responding and reacting. In session two there is still a Sender (Partner A), but Partner B is no longer a Receiver. He or she now agrees to be a *Listener* by doing two things: *responding* and *reacting*. The communication model now looks something like this:

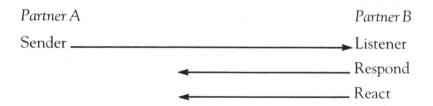

Partner A   *Partner B*

Sender ———————————————————▶ Listener

                    ◀——————————————— Respond

                    ◀——————————————— React

At this point, the distinction is made between responding and reacting. *Responding* is when a partner intently listens to the message sent and then repeats back what he or she has heard. *Reacting* is a comment, statement, or commentary about the message received.

Going back to our couple, Richard wants to be Sender and Paula has agreed to be Listener. Richard sends his message, which might go something like this: "Paula, I appreciate the meals you cook, but I'm getting a little bit tired of tuna fish casserole. We seem to have it two or three times a week."

Paula may want to lash out at Richard for criticizing her cooking. Isn't he aware that she works until five o'clock each day while he is in school, and she doesn't have time to cook elaborate meals? If Paula were to say something like this, she would be reacting rather than responding. As a rule in the second session, partners should try to respond to a message before reacting to it.

Paula could first respond, "Richard, you're saying I'm not a very good cook and you don't like my tuna fish casserole. Is that correct?" The two partners should clarify the message, restating it if necessary, until Partner A feels his or her message is clearly understood.

In our example, Richard did not actually say Paula was not a good cook. In fact, he had paid her a compliment by saying he appreciated her meals. And he did not say he did not like tuna fish casserole. He just didn't like it as often as Paula cooked it. Paula should continue to respond by repeating back the message until Richard believes she understands what he has said.

After she has responded, Paula may then react to the message by telling Richard how she feels about what he said. She might react by describing her busy schedule and how she thought he liked tuna fish casserole because he always ate it when she fixed it. And she might even say that she is afraid to experiment with untried recipes because of lack of confidence in her cooking skills. All of these statements come under the reacting category.

By distinguishing between responding and reacting, husband and wives can avoid many misunderstandings. Much of what we call conversation is nothing more than simultaneous monologues. We really don't listen to, or in fact may not even care about, what the other person is saying because we are so caught up in our desire to be heard or understood. All we are doing during these "conversations" is getting our next speech ready. Our thoughts and words are often pre-planned.

But if we learn to respond before reacting, if we tried to listen and understand what the other is saying, we might want to change what we would eventually say. But most of us want to be understood by our husband or wife more than we want to understand them.

Session three: Staying on the topic. How often in marital communication do we skip from topic to topic, from issue to issue, and never really go into depth on any one item? Rather than spending one hour discussing eight or ten different issues, would it not be better to spend fifteen or twenty minutes discussing just one in depth and agreeing on some action to take?

After Partner B (Listener) has responded and then reacted to the original message, the model of communication has changed and we now have:

Once Partner B reacts, he or she then becomes Sender and Partner A the Listener who, in turn, will respond and then react to the message sent by Partner B.

Paula might react to Richard's message by talking about how busy she is, her fear of cooking new recipes, and her fear of his criticism. And Richard might be tempted to say "Oh, you're so self-conscious," or, "How could you be more busy than I am?" If Richard were to do this, he would be reacting, not responding.

To first respond, he might say something like, "Paula, I

hear you saying you fix tuna casserole so much because you think I like it. Also, you say you like cooking foods you know how to cook to avoid any risk of failure or hearing me complain. Is that what you're saying, Paula?" If Paula says "Yes, that's what I said," Richard has responded and is then free to react to what she said. And thus the model continues back and forth.

Another rule of communication in session three is to leave the topic only when the original sender agrees to do so. For instance, Paula might feel uncomfortable talking about her tuna fish casseroles, so she may try to change the topic of conversation by complaining that Richard has not repaired the bathroom cabinet drawer that he promised to fix two weeks ago. While this may be an issue for her, it is not appropriate for her to bring it up now to evade the tuna fish casserole issue.

After they have resolved that issue, Paula could start a new conversation about the drawer. Richard might agree to hear what she has to say by being a Receiver (session one), or he might even agree to be a Listener (session two). By agreeing to listen, however, he commits himself to say something back to Paula, and hopefully he will remember to respond before reacting.

Richard might be threatened by his failure to fix the bathroom drawer and want, as did Paula, to change the topic or even ignore the message once Paula sends it. Using this model of communication, however, he would agree to stay on the topic (session three) of the bathroom drawer and discuss it until the original sender, Paula, is satisfied she has been heard and some appropriate action will be taken.

In summary, the Schuable-Hill Communication Exercise teaches the following simple but effective concepts in marital communication:

1. The partners identify one sender and one listener at a time.

2. The partners distinguish between listening and receiving.

3. The sender should state a clear message and the listener repeat it until the message is understood.

4. The listener should learn to respond before reacting.

5. The partners leave the topic of conversation only when the original sender agrees to do so.

For more information about communication skills in marriage you may want to read *Marriage* by Spencer W. Kimball, *Marriage: Much More Than a Dream* by Rex A. Skidmore, *The Marriage Dialogue* by Lynn Scoresby, *How to Strengthen and Improve Your Marriage* by Hugh Allred, *Peoplemaking* by Virginia Satir, and *Alive and Aware, Improving Communication in Relationships* by Sherod Miller, Elam Nunnally, and Daniel Wackman.

Communication exercises available at Brigham Young University are *The Interpersonal Game* by Kenneth Hardy, and the CHEC *Program* (Couples Handbook for Effective Communication) by Hugh Allred. These two exercises are self-explanatory and can be completed at home.

Bridges or Walls?

Richard B. Wilke claims in his book *Tell Me Again, I'm Listening*[9] that communication between husband and wife is the key to a fulfilling marriage. In addition, he believes that effective communication in marriage is not easy to attain. Wilke says, "Trying to understand each other in marriage is tough. It's a goal that has to be pursued relentlessly. The task is one that never ends. It's like golf. Just about the time you think you have got the game in hand, you slice one into the trees or blow a simple putt. You never totally win. You work at it. As in most other important things in life, you may succeed today but you have to do it again tomorrow."

To illustrate his point, Wilke relates that some friends of his who have a great marriage are keenly aware of the difficulties of communication. The husband is a busy doctor; the wife is the mother of several small children. Just to remind themselves of the importance of communication in marriage, they have a motto on their kitchen wall: "I know you believe you understand what you think I said, but I am not sure you realize that what you heard is not what I meant."

Wilke says that communication is to love what blood is to

22

the body. When communication stops, love dies and resentment and hate are born. To communicate means to be willing and able to learn from each other. It assumes that someone else has something significant to say. Most of us are ready to give answers before questions are completely asked or understood. Communication simply means we take the other person and what he or she has to say seriously.

Communication also means a certain kind of discipline. On occasion, we may have to hold our tongue. Or, it may mean forcing ourselves to say something as a response when we don't feel like saying it.

Communication also means openness. Since both husband and wife are constantly changing, their understanding of each other requires constant evaluation. As marriage partners change, it is as if they are symbolically shooting at moving targets while they are on the move themselves. Wilke concludes, "Marriages in which individuals build impenetrable walls around themselves are sick. 'I just can't get through to him (or her)' are words of frustration."

Marriage partners have before them the bricks and mortar of communication. With these materials, they can build bridges to or walls between each other. What they build is up to the couple.

2

LOVE

Love is one important aspect of marriage. Most people will not marry and stay married unless they both love and feel loved by their partner. It is not surprising, therefore, that wives expect husbands to express love in their marriage. In fact, expressing love was ranked number two in the "Profile of a Loving Husband."

What Love Is

There have been many attempts to define love. Plato cynically described it as "a grave mental disease." Thomas Carlyle noted that "love is not altogether a delirium, yet it has many points in common therewith." Helen Rowland simply described love as "woman's eternal spring and man's eternal fall." And according to John Barrymore, love is "the delightful interval between meeting a beautiful girl and discovering that she looks like a haddock." Samuel Johnson said, "Love is the wisdom of the fool and the folly of the wise." George Bernard Shaw defined love as "the gross exaggeration of the difference between one person and everybody else." "Love is like the measles," said Josh Billings. "We can have it but once, and the later in life we have it, the tougher it goes with us." H. L. Mencken thought love to be "the delusion that one woman differs from another." Still another writer, unknown, defined love as "one hormone system calling to another." Other anonymous definitions of love are "an intoxication of the nervous system," "triumph of imagination over intelligence," and "a process that

24

turns a young woman's frog into a prince." Alphonse Karr wrote of love, "It is the most terrible, and also the most generous of passions: it is the only one which includes in its dreams the happiness of someone else." The poet Percy Bysshe Shelley wrote, "Love withers under constraint; its very essence is liberty; it is compatible neither with obedience, jealousy, nor fear." Henry Ward Beecher said, "Love is the river of life in this world. Think not that ye know of it who stand at the little tinkling rill, the first small fountain. Not until you have gone through the rocky gorges, and not lost the streams; not until you have gone through the meadow, and the stream has widened and deepened until the fleets could ride upon its bosom; not until beyond the meadow you have come to the unfathomable ocean, and poured your treasures into its depths —not until then can you know what love is."

These are but a few examples of the many definitions of love. And it really does not matter how many there are. The most important definitions of love are the ones assigned to it by two people in a relationship.

For some, "I love you" means "I want to be with you." It may mean "I want to control you," or "I trust you." In some instances, "I love you" means "I want to be intimate with you." Or, it could mean "I want to share your money with you."

In contemporary marriage, love is defined as having at least three components, emotion, behavior, and commitment.

Certainly, love is *emotion*. Most people describe love as some kind of emotional experience where two people identify with each other. William Goode, a sociologist, defined love as "a strong emotional attachment between adolescents or adults of the opposite sexes with at least the components of sex desire and tenderness."[1] Historically, the Greeks had three different words to describe the emotions often associated with love. *Eros* referred to sexual or romantic love; *agape* was related to selfless, altruistic, caring love; *philos* referred to brotherly or fraternal love.

Love is *behavior*. In 1 Corinthians 13, Paul lists fourteen characteristics that Christians through the centuries have come to identify with love. (See chapter 5 on spirituality.)

Showing love by behavior is what his book is all about. In

addition to telling a wife that he loves her, what can a husband do to show it? The answer to that question is the answer to this one: "What does his wife expect?"

Love is *commitment*. This is very important. Too frequently we think of love only as emotion or behavior. If we were to base our love only on these, our attractions and attachment to each other would depend only on the momentary emotions we feel or the behaviors we experience with our spouses. If our emotions are bland and the behavior questionable, then we may feel unloved or loved less.

If commitment is perceived as a vital component of love, then love will survive ulcers, the absence of make-up, wrinkles, gray hair, or even baldness. Love will also withstand variations in weight; it will not be measured by inches around the waist or the weight on the scales. Including commitment as part of love will help us endure the highs and lows on the roller coaster ride of marital emotions.

Perhaps that is what most wedding vows imply when people marry "in sickness and in health, for richer or for poorer, and for better or for worse." When sickness, poverty, and bad times come, the relationship will survive because the partners are committed to each other. That, indeed, is true love.

Types of Love

Specific types or "styles" of love have recently been described by Dr. Carlfred Broderick in his book *Marriage and the Family*.[2] Following is a model of his "types" and definitions with slight adaptations:

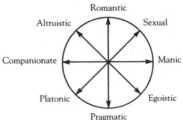

The eight types represented in the circle are in four pairs of opposites with the following definitions:

Romantic love is usually emotional, often irrational, and sometimes based solely on sexual attraction. It usually encompasses strong desires to be near, touch, care for, and share experiences with the loved one. There is strong commitment to each other or to the relationship. A romantic lover also often idealizes the loved one or the place or situation in which they find themselves.

Sexual love is often part of romantic love but can be experienced with little or no romantic attachment. Sexual or erotic love is one important part of establishing intimacy between a married couple. (See chapter three on intimacy.)

Manic love is the idealization of a loved one with intense emotions, sometimes to the point of being all-consuming. Sleep, hunger, and common concerns of everyday life are replaced by passion. Common characteristics of manic love are extreme joy and despair, with the tendency to be possessive rather than caring, and clinging rather than giving.

Egoistic love is self-serving or competitive love. In an extreme form, it is detrimental to marriage. Yet, some relationships enjoy a matching of wits and playful competition, where egoistic love is very important. Enough of this style is needed in marriage to protect the interests of the individuals involved.

Pragmatic love (opposite of romantic love) is highly rational, practical, and not very intense. Pragmatic lovers have a limited need to touch, care for, or be with a loved person.

Platonic love (opposite of sexual love) involves little or no sexual interaction in the marital relationship. It is highly spiritual and free from sexual desire.

Companionate love (opposite of manic love) emphasizes friendship and loyalty, and only gradually takes on romantic overtones. Disagreements and periods of separation are easily survived. It is stable, non-demanding, committed, and trusting, but also lacks the drama, intensity, and mood swings of manic love.

Altruistic love (opposite of egoistic love) is being kind, caring, and sensitive to a partner's needs. But it can be destructive if little is required in return. A person in this love style will often pass up opportunities for more personal fulfillment. They may appear to be saintly. However, they lack the self-preservation value of egoistic love. Demanding nothing but the opportunity to serve, altruistic lovers are often taken advantage of.

Of these love types, Broderick notes: "We can see no single formula is ideal. Rather a case can be made that the most successful mixtures are those types which are not extreme in any one direction."[3]

In summary, most happily married couples tend to have a balance rather than a preoccupation with any of the styles of love. It is also likely that each of the types contributes something of value to a marriage and that conversely each type alone, or in combinations of one or two, is enough to sufficiently strengthen the marital bond.

Love Intensity Varies

Some married couples, particularly newlyweds, become unduly concerned because they experience hills and valleys in their emotional intensity. They assume that because they feel less emotionally intense toward each other at times that something must be wrong.

Not long ago, I was in a counseling session with a young man and woman who had been married just a few months. They had come to see me because after a recent fight she accused him of not loving her anymore. It was discouraging to them that their relationship could seemingly deteriorate to this level after just a few months of marriage.

I explained to them that we often think of love as all or nothing. Supposedly, either we love our marriage partner or we don't. Or, we may decide that our spouse previously loved us but no longer does. (I have found even in many divorces that ex-husbands and wives still love each other in various ways.) Sometimes we also view love as an elusive butterfly—difficult to capture, magnificent after attaining, and extremely fragile upon possession.

After some conversation, I suggested to the young couple that they probably still loved each other (which they admitted), but that the intensity of their relationship may have slightly diminished after the initial rapture of the wedding and honeymoon. In fact, the young man and his new bride were probably entering phase 2 of marriage, as described by Dr. Abraham and Dorothy Schmitt at the University of Pennsylvania. (See chapter seven on autonomy, pp. 111-20.)

Few married couples always feel the same high emotional intensity toward each other, even though they may be deeply committed to their relationship. Events and circumstances outside the relationship may also demand the interest and attention of a husband or wife. Subsequently, his or her marriage partner may feel they are competing with these events for their spouse's time and interest. Jobs, college, children, parents, hobbies, and involvement in community and church activities are among the competitors that may cause a husband or wife to feel ignored or "unloved."

During the married years, the intensity of the emotions will vary up and down, even if it is ever so slight. And it is during these times of "down" that we frequently feel unloved or accuse the other of not loving just because we feel the intensity less.

Dr. James Dobson, author of *What Wives Wish Their Husbands Knew About Women*,[4] has asked, "How many vulnerable young couples 'fall in love' with love on the first date . . . and lock themselves in marriage before the natural swing of their emotions has even progressed through the first dip? They then wake up one morning without that neat feeling and conclude that love has died. In reality, it was never there in the first place. They were fooled by an emotional high." (P. 90.)

Dr. Dobson further notes, "Even when a man and woman love each other deeply and genuinely they will find themselves supercharged on one occasion and emotionally bland on another. However, their love is not defined by the highs and lows, but it is dependent on a commitment of their will." (P. 91.)

Love intensity also varies during times of confrontation in marriage. Many married couples not only become annoyed at each other, but they also become disappointed because they believe happily married couples do not "fight" or ever get angry at each other. In an article, "Little Problems of Married Life,"[5] William George Jordan said: "Those married people who tell me, ten or fifteen years after the wedding, that there never has been one cross word spoken between them, never a moment of even irritation, never a single shadowing cloud of disagreement, belong to one of three classes: They have been mercifully endowed with a talent for forgetting, they handle truth with a

29

certain shyness, or one of them is the overawed victim of the other's personality." (P. 787.)

Jordan then makes an interesting analogy: "Have you ever heard an old sea-captain boast that in all his experience he had never seen a squally sea, never a dull, heavy storm-laden sky, never heard the tempest shriek through the rigging, then threaten to tear away the masts? His pride is in his skill, not in his luck. The matrimonial sea never remains absolutely serene and calm, with no ruffling waves for years at a time. The vital point is that the storms have all been weathered in safety, and the love and trust, purified by time, remain undaunted." (P. 788.)

The intriguing aspect of this quotation is that it was made in 1910, more than seventy years ago.

It has been estimated that only fifty percent of behavior in marriage is based on reason and intellect. The other half of what we do is an outgrowth of our emotions. We often disregard the fact that we, as husband and wife, are as yet imperfect and susceptible to mood swings, and that even temple marriages require constant attention and effort. By ignoring our emotions, we create illusions of what marriage is like. And it is the false ideas of marriage that cause disillusionment or even divorce.

Perhaps contemporary marriage would seem less disconcerting if we would reexamine some of the false ideas we have about it, such as "There is no conflict in a good marriage." If we could realize that most husbands and wives do, on occasion, become emotionally charged, we might be less upset when it occurs. Maybe then we could get on with the business of dealing with our emotions rather than denying we have them in the first place. And remembering in the process that we still love each other.

How to Express Your Love

As noted in the "Profile of a Loving Husband," wives frequently expect a husband to show his love by word and by deeds. This was also borne out in the many letters from wives indicating at least four ways love might be conveyed: (1) verbal expression, (2) written expression, (3) doing deeds, and (4) gifts.

Verbal Expression

There once was an elderly wife who complained to her aging husband that he seldom told her he loved her. "I told you I loved you when we first got married," he responded angrily, "and if anything changes, you'll be the first to know."

As absurd as this story may seem, it is amazing how infrequently many husbands say to their wives those three little words, "I love you." It takes about three seconds, and most wives not only want it, but expect it.

One wife wrote, "We wives all love being told we are loved and appreciated—a husband just can't do too much of this."

Still another woman said, "More than anything else, I would like my husband to express verbally what it is he loves about me and tell me that he loves me more often. I need that verbal reassurance as the days go by; I need to be told more than once or twice with the assumption that I will just know it for the rest of my life."

Apparently, some men say "I love you," but in a sarcastic way. One wife said, "I wish he could tell me he loved me without putting a joke or laugh with it. He just can't say it seriously."

Most women know they are loved, and all they need is reassurance. Sometimes it is just better to be reminded than to be informed. "I need the reassurance of his loyalty to me," one wife said, "both in words and actions." Similarly, another said, "Verbal expression (a real event would be to have it written!) is important, not just "I love you," but expression of specific appreciation for me as a person and what I accomplish in life."

Most wives need verbal expression from their husbands to assure them of continuing love and security. A husband should be wise enough to know this about his wife and loving enough to do it. He can build her self-esteem just through his words to her. Words have power. A husband can show his love for his wife with a card or candy or flowers. But by all means, say it with words.

31

Written Expression

When speaking is difficult or impossible, another effective means of communication is to write your feelings on paper and share them with a loved one. One wife wrote:

> "My husband makes me feel very close to him when he buys me a greeting card. But, he doesn't leave it at that—he writes something extra inside that sincerely expresses a feeling he has that the greeting doesn't convey. Just a few extra words to let me know that he loves me deeply are appreciated. Some men seem to be afraid of saying or writing what they term 'mush.' But they would be surprised what effect it could have on their relationship with their wife. If they would dig down deep in their heart and let some of that love out, most marriages would improve greatly."

One woman said, "I enjoy receiving a small personal gift occasionally or even a love note scribbled on the back of an old envelope. It seems that life is too busy and all we do is attend to the necessary chores and the day is gone too soon."

Another woman wrote, "Three years ago, after a particularly difficult move (aren't they all!), he wrote me a note thanking me for many of the things I have done. I still have the note. And last year he wrote a page of reasons 'Why I Love Karen.' That page is like gold to me."

I have personally found conveying love in writing to be very rewarding. It has always been difficult for me on Valentine's Day to go down to the drugstore and buy my wife a valentine. For one thing, I always get there late and the cards are pretty well picked over or there are just one or two left on the floor with footprints on them. And I feel that what is written in cards is rather impersonal. It is wrong, I think, to always let someone else express your feelings for you.

When we were engaged, I was confused about love and had difficulty expressing how I felt toward Susan. Conveying my love was difficult because I really didn't know what to say except "I love you."

On the Valentine's Day before we were married, I sat up all night and wrote Susan a long poem, one of my first, titled

"Love, Undefined." I gave it to her on Valentine's Day, along with a wrinkled commercial card, and she was impressed, or at least she acted like it. Anyway, she still has the poem in a scrapbook, which impresses me. But writing my thoughts down during a confusing time in our relationsip was helpful to me, and I think it conveyed something of my love to her.

A few years after we were married, I suggested, and Susan agreed, that rather than buying the commercial cards on Valentine's Day, we would make our own and then write a few lines in them. I have enjoyed doing this and appreciate the cards I get from her. I hope she feels the same way about mine.

Doing Deeds

Husbands can talk about love all day, every day, but if they fail to *do* something to show their love, their wives may doubt their sincerity.

One wife expressed it well: "Saying 'I love you,' of course, is great to hear, but I like actions rather than words. My husband can say he loves me until he's blue in the face, but if he acts as though it is a great burden to do things for me, his love is in doubt."

Another said, "I guess the biggest thing, in my opinion, a husband can do to show his love and appreciation for his wife is not bringing candy, flowers, or that kind of thing, but just doing things to *show* her that she is important."

Following are some comments by appreciative wives:

"My husband has done many things around the house so that my daily chores could be done more efficiently. He put shelves in the fruit room, made a long folding table in the laundry area, put a board with hooks along a wall for the children to hang coats on, and put up another board in their bedroom with hooks on which to hang their sacks and toys. These actions demonstrated that he heard, understood, and loved me enough to help make my work easier."

"Recently I left home early to fill a church assignment. While I was gone, my husband made the bed, vacuumed the bedroom carpet, and washed a large picture window (one I have a nightmare trying to clean)—all before he went to work. Did that ever tell me he loves me!"

"I appreciate it when he pitches in and helps me instead of just watching me work. He'll dry the dishes or help with dinner or get the kids ready for bed. I am also grateful when he helps with breakfast on the weekends. And occasionally he has helped me bottle fruit. Now these things don't happen very often, but when they do, it thrills me to think he cares enough to do them."

"The ways he shows me he loves me are by giving a helping hand with the kids, helping with the house-work if I get in a bind, or especially taking time to listen with an understanding heart. Doing things for me means much more than the words 'I love you,' although I appreciate him saying that frequently also."

"My husband has a real hard time saying, 'I love you,' but he shows me in a hundred ways. For example, if I lie down in the day, he tip-toes around, he shares the housework, he opens the car door for me, he takes my arm to cross the street, and he never belittles me or picks an argument. He is just a great husband and we are seventy and seventy-one years old. That is love enough for me!"

One young wife said, "It isn't that men don't know how to love women. It's that people don't know how to love people. We tend to do for them what would make us happy if someone would do it for us. And then we wonder why the other person isn't happy. After all, it would make us happy, so it has to be right."

Many men, as she noted, so some things for their wives to show love. But how do wives get husbands to do the things they want them to do? Dr. W. Robert Beavers, director of the Southwest Family Institute in Dallas, Texas, may have the an-swer. Writing in a publication of the American Association of Marriage and Family Therapists, Dr. Beavers, on a rather humorous note, said that wives are always trying to get husbands to do something: be more affectionate, pick up their clothes, and so on. In his article, "Lessons From a Dancing Chicken,"[6] he notes, "I frequently tell a story about an Arkansas boy who went north and ran into a fellow named B. F. Skinner, who taught him how to make a chicken do three things: dance, play baseball, and ride a fire engine. Such wondrous knowledge should be shared so he went back to Arkansas and opened up an establishment called the I. Q. Zoo, a display of fabulous animal feats. Now if an ordinary person can make a chicken dance, surely you can get your husband to _____ (fill in the blank). It's a matter of knowing how."

First, says Dr. Beavers, you must believe that the chicken isn't evil, and isn't making every attempt to thwart your hopes and dreams. It's hard to train a chicken that you think has it in for you.

Second, you must reward the chicken with something the chicken likes, not what you think he ought to like, nor with whatever's handy. (For humans, he notes, probably the most powerful reward is a moment of shared delight.)

Third, you must reward approximations of the behavior desired. If you wait until the chicken does the complete dance before rewarding it, you will wait a long time. A turn of the head to the left or a foot moving in the right direction should merit a quick reward.

Fourth, you must ignore behavior you don't want; it is called "undancing behavior." The combination of alert rewards and careful neglect of the unwanted is a powerful tool in producing a dancing chicken.

Fifth, punishment is not necessary, according to Dr. Beavers, in creating a dancing chicken. A starved chicken just doesn't dance nor do much of anything else very well. Without frequent rewards, punishment sometimes becomes perceived as a reward and encourages behavior it is supposed to diminish.

One can also ask the chicken to become a collaborator by discussing which rewards would be effective, helping to improve negotiating skills.

Dr. Beavers says one more element is needed; a rule must be imposed: The responsibility for change and the desire for change must be kept within the same person. This makes it clear who is chicken and who is trainer at a given time.

This rule plus the five steps in teaching a chicken to dance can help many husbands and wives break frustrating patterns and build satisfying ones. If you can get a chicken to dance, you ought to be able to get your husband to take out the garbage once in a while. And all it might take is a little peck on the cheek now and then.

Giving Gifts

Apparently, giving a gift symbolically conveys love to many wives. And it is, indeed, a symbol. But a gift is cheap no matter the amount paid for it, if a husband is not willing to give of himself, his time, his affection, his appreciation, or his thoughts to his wife. Many men believe buying frequent and often expensive gifts for their wives will suffice for expressions of love. It was interesting in the "Profile of a Loving Husband" that "He brings me unexpected gifts, flowers, and cards and sometimes writes a note attached to the gift," something judged by many husbands to be important, received relatively low ranking by wives. In fact, only six percent of the wives listed gifts in their top five priorities. And when ranked, it was often only eighth, ninth, or tenth, indicating many other things were more important. Wives simply cannot be appeased with gifts. Of the twenty items listed in the "Profile of a Loving Husband," seventeen received a higher ranking than did giving gifts.

Nevertheless, gifts are important in that the absence of gifts often communicates inattentiveness, unconcern, or a general withdrawal of feelings. One wife said, "Of course, all wives like little gifts and surprises brought home for no reason at all, other than to show love."

And another said, "For anniversaries and birthdays, instead of going out to eat, I would appreciate personal gifts. It would make me feel 'remembered.' "

And gifts don't have to be either practical or expensive. In fact, one wife wrote, "Why does a husband have to always give 'practical' gifts like toasters or irons or food slicers? Why can't he buy something more personal than an appliance I 'need.'

And, by the way, a gift doesn't have to cost a lot." Another wife echoed this sentiment: "In the future, I'll be as happy as the day I married him if he only remembers 'It's the little things that count.' And a gift that doesn't cost a penny can often make a woman feel like a million dollars."

But sometimes giving a gift of value is important. It is amazing to me how a husband cannot afford a five dollar gift for his wife, but somehow can come up with the money to buy a three-hundred-dollar rifle or fifty-dollar fishing rod for himself on sale at the local sporting goods store. A wife wrote, "One of the nicest gifts my husband ever gave me was a lovely, expensive music box that played one of our love songs. I was overwhelmed! It was a tender and long-remembered moment for both of us."

And sometimes, just silly, spontaneous gifts convey a great deal of love and caring. One such gift was described by a young college wife:

"As a full-time student and part-time worker, both my husband and I must share responsibility for taking care of our domestic needs. One day I had written out a grocery list, but never made it to the grocery store. The last item on the list was soft drinks (Fresca), and I had underlined it. I guess I had a craving for it. I was delighted that evening when I returned home from school and found that not only was the grocery shopping done, but in the middle of the living room floor was a large heart made out of forty-eight Fresca bottles. Although our budget couldn't really afford that much pop, our marriage certainly needed that extra sparkle."

Of all the gifts mentioned, flowers were given most frequently and were apparently most appreciated. It seems essential, therefore, that husbands learn to understand "flower power" in conveying love.

Consider the importance of flowers as shown in the following quotations:

"In the future, my husband could remember how important birthdays are to me, and throw a surprise party for me. We could also go out to dinner for no reason at

37

all, or he could be more romantic by surprising me with flowers.

"Husbands should remember little things such as candy, a poem, flowers, or anything of dating days. Some of the important things my husband could do to show his love would be leaving cards or notes, or calling me from work or school to say he loves me, or bringing flowers home."

And apparently many husbands do give their wives flowers. One wrote, "For my birthday, my husband sent me an arrangement of real flowers. I was so pleased I took pictures of it so I could always remember it."

A mother with a large family wrote, "At the birth of each child my husband brought me a flower, one for each child we had. So when our twelfth child was born, I received a dozen red roses."

One young wife wrote, "Occasionally, my husband brings me one flower, for no reason at all!"

My father wrote a poem about a rose just a few months after my mother died. She and my father had grown roses in their garden and had frequently exchanged a rose "for no reason at all" other than to express their love for each other. In his poem, "One Rose," Dad helps husbands better understand the power of a flower.

One Rose
You surely recall youth's sweet moments:
The stars and the moon shone so bright
As you wined her and dined her to music
With a bouquet of roses each night.

It was, oh, such a beautiful courtship;
You kissed her full lips and pink cheek
    And sighed in her ear,
    "I love you, my dear."
There were orchids or roses each week.

The honeymoon deepened your romance
As you pledged your true love once again.

LOVE

This bond would not sever;
You'd love her forever.
There were pansies and pinks now and then.

Then came babies, the bottles, the budget;
And things just didn't seem to go right:
But don't you suppose
She still needed a rose
And a kiss on a Saturday night?

There was cooking, and sewing, and cleaning
While time itself seemed to take flight.
The work's never done;
Still she longs for some fun
And one rose on a Saturday night.

You declare love with gifts when expected—
Anniversaries and each Christmas Night—
But some people say
There's a much better way:
Try a rose on a Saturday night.

As the years pass, we all grow neglectful:
Hold her hand; touch her lips; hold her tight.
As life ebbs to a close,
She still longs for a rose.
Bring a fresh one this Saturday night.

One day when your sweetheart has left you,
You will have God's own word she's all right.
When the spring breezes stir
Fragrant memories of her,
Press a rose to your lips every night.

—Alvin R. Barlow

3

INTIMACY

It became clear in the "Profile of a Loving Husband" and from the numerous letters received from women that wives want to be close physically, mentally, emotionally, and spiritually to their husbands.

In his book *Love-Life*[1], Dr. Ed Wheat has a chapter titled "The Secret of Staying in Love." In it, he notes, "It is a remarkable fact that while millions of men and women have no difficulty falling in love, at least half of that number seem unable to stay in love. The secret of staying in love for any couple . . . is a life long love affair. The secret in one potent word is *intimacy*." (P. 130.)

Often when we hear the word "intimacy" we think only of sexual intimacy. While this is part of it, intimacy is much more than sexual relationships. Listed below are some of the strands, according to Dr. Wheat, that make up the bonds of intimacy between husband and wife. They are in no particular order, and each couple may have others of their own to add.

Intimacy Bonds

Physical touching of an affectionate, non-sexual nature
Shared feelings
Closeness without inhibitions

Absence of psychological defenses
Open communication and honesty
Intellectual agreement on major issues
Spiritual harmony
Sensitive appreciation of the mate's physical and
     emotional responses
Similar values held
Imparted secrets
Genuine understanding
Mutual confidence
A sense of warmth, safety, and relaxation when together
Sexual pleasures lovingly shared
Signs of love freely given and received
Mutual responsibility and caring
Abiding trust

The Need for Touch

Two dominant trends became evident in the "Profile of a Loving Husband." Wives want affection and touch in addition to fulfillment through sexual relationships. And they want it in that order.

Item 7 of "Profile of a Loving Husband" was: "He expresses affection by touch without sexual overtones." Item 4 was "He helps me attain sexual satisfaction in our relationship." It is interesting that item 7 was consistently rated higher than item 4, suggesting that touch and affection are as important, if not more important, than sexual relationships. What most husbands do not realize is that touch and affection for most wives is sex!

It is obvious, therefore, that men and women often have differing perspectives of sexuality in marriage. While men often see sex as intercourse, women usually view sex as the preliminaries.

Many husbands do not understand that wives expect touch and affection without always having to head straight to bed. Yet that was consistently reported by many wives. For instance, one wife wrote, "My husband and I have a rewarding and mutually satisfying sexual relationship so it is not like I get tired of the activity because I do enjoy it. But there are times when I would like to be close and have him hold me without going beyond that. Sometimes when I am tired, I'd rather just go to sleep in his arms."

Another wife wrote: "Not long ago my husband did just a little thing, but it sure made my day. He put his arms around me, kissed me, and said, 'How I love you!' This was not a prelude to making love or having me do anything in particular for him. It just made me feel great!"

One appreciative wife noted, "My husband shows his affection by putting his arm around me, smiling at me, hugging me, and holding my hands, especially in places other than in the bedroom."

But it is apparently very difficult for many men to be affectionate by touch without sexual overtones. In *Love-Life*, Dr. Ed Wheat emphasizes the importance of husbands touching their wives in non-sexual ways.

He notes:

> A tender touch tells us that we are cared for. It can calm our fears, soothe pain, bring us comfort, or give us the blessed satisfaction of emotional security. As adults, touching continues to be a primary means of communicating with those we love, whether we are conscious of it or not. Our need for a caring touch is normal and healthy and we will never outgrow it.
>
> But if touching is so valuable and pleasurable, why is it necessary to advise couples to do more of it? The answer lies in our culture. While our western civilization is highly sexual, it frowns on or ignores touching apart from sex. This is particularly true for men, for there are only three acceptable kinds of touching in today's world: the superficial handshake, aggressive contact sports, and the sexual encounter. Men have been conditioned to turn to sex whenever they feel any need for loving closeness. No wonder experts believe that our extreme preoccupation with sex in this society

is actually an expression of our deep, unsatisfied need for the warmth, reassurance, and intimacy of non-sexual touching.

Physical contact is absolutely essential in building the emotion of love. *Anything else you do will be of little avail unless you learn to touch each other often and joyfully in non-sexual ways.* If you would like to kindle a flame in your own marriage, then begin to show your love through physical touching. (Pp. 183-84; italics added.)

Sexual Fulfillment Desired

The second part of intimacy is that wives want and seek fulfillment with their husbands in the sexual relationship itself. This finding is consistent with a recent report by Paul Ammons and Nick Stinnet who studied seventy-two happily married couples in Oklahoma. The couples were mostly rural, middle-aged, middle-income people who had been married between fifteen and twenty-five years. The number of children varied from two to twelve.

In their article "The Vital Marriage: A Closer Look,"[2] Stinnet and Ammons reported that one thing these seventy-two couples had in common was that fulfilling sexual relationships were found to be a central and profoundly important part of their marriages. A majority, eighty-five percent of the respondents, reported moderately high to very high needs for sexual fulfillment. This suggests that for these happily married couples, and undoubtedly others, sexual fulfillment is an important component of marriage and a major way of sustaining intimacy in their relationship. The similar high need for sexual fulfillment was found equally in husbands and wives.

I might add that in all my years of marriage counseling, I have never found a marriage that was satisfying and stable unless both husband and wife were deriving sexual satisfaction from the relationship. This need for sexual satisfaction was also reported in our surveys and letters:

"My husband is very concerned that he pleases and satisfies me in love-making. In fact, he seems to find his greatest pleasure in making the experience a delightful and pleasurable one for me, in making sure that I truly enjoy it. This has just thrilled me, that he is concerned about me and not just interested in satisfying himself."

"My husband is a patient, considerate, and creative lover who finds pleasure in helping me find sexual fulfillment."

But apparently there is need for improvement in some sexual relationships. One wishful wife noted, "I wish he would take the time to sexually arouse me, so I could enjoy being close to him."

Another wife related, "I would greatly appreciate it if my husband would grab me, carry me off to the bedroom, and make love to me. Our sexual relationship needs improvement!"

If sexual fulfillment is not attained immediately in some marriages, and there is some evidence that it is not, married couples should note that it is something they can look forward to. A recent survey of over one hundred thousand readers of *Redbook* magazine found that most couples married for several years reported a satisfying sex life. About thirty-three percent rated the sexual aspect of their marriage as "very good," and another thirty-four percent rated it as "good." Thus, two-thirds of those reporting were satisfied with their sexual relationship. Only twenty-one percent rated their sexual relationship as "fair," and the remaining twelve percent stated it was either "poor" or "very poor."[3] So the odds for sexual fulfillment in marriage are good.

But if sexual fulfillment is not found immediately, the couple need not become distraught. Like other dimensions of a satisfying marriage, sexual fulfillment does not come automatically; it requires some effort.

An LDS Perspective

One of the first Church leaders to write at length on the subject of intimacy was Parley P. Pratt. In an essay entitled "Intelligence and Affection,"[4] Elder Pratt noted:

44

Some persons have supposed that our natural affections were the results of a fallen and corrupt nature, and that they are "carnal, sensual, and devilish," and therefore ought to be resisted, subdued, or overcome as so many evils which prevent our perfection, or progress in the spiritual life. . . . Our natural affections are planted in us by the Spirit of God, for a wise purpose; and they are the very main-springs of life and happiness—they are the cement of all virtuous and heavenly society—they are the essence of charity, or love; and therefore never fail, but endure forever. There is not a more pure and holy principle in existence than the affection which glows in the bosom of a virtuous man for his companion.

The fact is, God made man, male and female; he planted in their bosoms those affections which are calculated to promote their happiness and union. That by that union they might fulfill the first and great commandment, . . . "To multiply and replenish the earth, and subdue it." From this union of affection, springs all the other relationships, social joys and affections diffused through every branch of human existence. And were it not for this, earth would be a desert wild, and uncultivated wilderness.

On a similar note, Elder Hugh B. Brown wrote in his book *You and Your Marriage:*[5]

Sex is not an unmentionable human misfortune, and certainly it should not be regarded as a sordid but necessary part of marriage. There is no excuse for approaching this most intimate relationship in life without true knowledge of its meaning and its high purpose. This is an urge which more insistently than others calls for self-control and intelligence. (P. 76.)

Elder Brown also noted:

Thousands of young people come to the marriage altar almost illiterate insofar as this basic and fundamental function is concerned. The sex instinct is not something which we need to fear or be ashamed of. It is God-given and has a high and holy purpose. (P. 73.)

Because so many newlyweds are apparently uninformed about sexual matters in marriage, Elder Brown counseled, "If the partners would discuss together *before marriage* the serious problems involved therein, . . . if they would frankly discuss the delicate and sanctifying aspects of harmonious sex life which are involved in marriage . . . , much sorrow, heartbreak, and tragedy could be avoided." (P. 21; italics added.)

Prerogative or Duty?

Certainly the decade of the '70s will be remembered for many things, including the reexamination and redefining of relationships between men and women. During the past few years, many people have become more sensitive to women in general and sexuality in particular. At the end of the decade, however, one wonders how long many of the myths and stereotypes about women and sexuality will be perpetuated. Among these many beliefs is the long-held tradition that sex is a man's prerogative and a woman's duty.

Prerogative means "an exclusive right or privilege exercised by virtue of rank or office; a right or privilege limited to a specific person, or persons of a particular category." The idea prevails that women are the sexual playthings of men, that sexual interaction in marriage is to be at the whim and desire of the husband. The only obligation of the wife, supposedly, is to meet his sexual demands as they are made.

In her book, *The Future of Marriage*,[6] Jessie Bernard notes that the relationship between many husbands and wives is being reexamined in what she described as the "His" and "Hers" perspective of marriage. Dr. Bernard suggests that two people in marriage can have the same experience and yet have entirely different perceptions of the experience. What may be meaningful and fulfilling for one may not be for the other. She also states that just because a husband enjoys a sexual relationship is

46

no guarantee that his wife will enjoy it at all. The sociologist observed that many contemporary males may have to learn more about female sexuality if marriage is going to be a viable relationship in the future.

The motives for sexual relationships in marriage are also believed to vary. The notion that men give love to get sex and women give sex to get love is yet another example of a sexual myth that still exists. This may be true for some, but need not be for all.

The belief that sex is something with which women placate men is fostered in many of the so-called men's magazines. There has recently been much controversy about the erotic photographs in these publications, but many marriage counselors and family life educators are equally concerned about the sexual philosophies advocated in much of the reading materials for men.

Professor J. Richard Udry of the University of North Carolina notes in his text *The Social Context of Marriage*[7] that much of the literature for men enforces the idea that women are sexually subservient. Dr. Udry observes that more than one hundred men's magazines are directed specifically at arousing sexual fantasies in males. Men, he claims, learn to view all women as having an unusually high sexual orientation, while this may be true of only ten to fifteen percent. These magazines, according to Professor Udry, reflect the stereotype of the hypersexual female waiting to fulfill the sexual demands and fantasies of males. Many men, unfortunately, have similar expectations of their wives.

Dr. Udry notes other sexual myths are perpetuated in magazines for males. Many of the publications depict only extremely beautiful women with a certain physique. This suggests that such women are the only ones capable of sexual interaction. Not all women, he states, are as attractive as those in the magazines nor do they all have the same body type. This does not mean they cannot have fulfilling sexual relationships.

Marriage could be more meaningful if sexual fulfillment were sought and experienced by both husband and wife. The idea that sex is a man's prerogative and a woman's duty has been believed too long by too many. Perhaps the time has come when sexual interaction in marriage can be an enjoyable prerogative for both.

The Early Years of Marriage

A few months ago, I spoke to a group of young married couples about the sexual dimensions of marriage. After my talk, a few couples came up with a question or two and then left. One couple, however, stayed until everyone else had gone and then hesitantly came over as I walked toward the door. They asked if I could stay a few minutes longer and answer a few questions for them.

I agreed and about that time the young wife started to cry. They said they had been married less than a year and thus far she had not been able to find much sexual fulfillment. They loved each other very much, but had found sexual intimacy to be frustrating. Their honeymoon, they said, had been a disaster.

The couple had sought counsel from a physician who advised them they probably wouldn't be able to achieve satisfaction for two or three more years and would just have to "wait it out." Such advice was of little comfort to the recently married couple.

I asked them a few questions about sexual fulfillment. It was soon evident that no one had ever asked them these questions before, let alone given them any answers. The problem, I ascertained, was that no one, including the physician, had informed them of some basic aspects of sexuality. I talked to them for about fifteen minutes, and they felt somewhat assured that there was still hope for them and their marriage. But their experience is all too common and unnecessary among newlyweds.

Many of the problems young couples experience with intimacy go back to their childhood and the things they were taught, or not taught, about sex. In accordance with gospel principles, young people should be taught to wait until marriage for sexual relationships. But they should also be taught to have a healthy and satisfying sexual relationship once they are married.

How we teach these matters seems to have particular significance for young women, because too many wives attain little or no sexual satisfaction in their marriages. Frigidity, the inability or unwillingness to find fulfillment in intimacy, is common in the United States. In his book *The Individual, Marriage, and the Family*,[8] Lloyd Saxton notes, "Frigidity is very common in our society, with one fourth of the married female population never having experienced orgasm by age twenty-five and as many as one in ten never experiencing it at any time during their married lives." (P. 79.)

Perhaps the inability of couples to make a successful sexual adjustment after marriage is due, in part, to many of the analogies we use to encourage young people to wait until marriage for sexual relationships. There is the chewed-up bubble gum, cake with the icing missing, and the nail, board, and nail hole, all of which must evoke some interesting images in the minds of young people. Another favorite is crushing a flower, such as a rose, and then asking young women if they want to be like bruised rose petals.

Young women are not flowers; they are normal human beings with strong biological and emotional inclinations toward intimacy. Crushing flowers in Seminary or Young Women's classes probably will not inhibit those feelings, and it will probably make them more confusing.

Rather than just saying "don't" and hoping they "won't," a more reasonable and effective approach may be to explain sexuality from a physical, social, mental, and spiritual perspective. This would help young people understand the problems associated with immorality as well as the blessings of intimacy in marriage.

Young people can be taught to be virtuous without being prudish. To be virtuous means to "conform to moral and ethical principles; [to be] morally excellent, upright, and chaste as a person." To be prudish, on the other hand, means to be "excessively proper or modest in speech, conduct, dress, etc." While I know many young men who would like to marry a virtuous young woman, and vice versa, I know of absolutely no one who wants to marry someone who is prudish.

We should teach young people about sexuality so that they have a healthy concept of it after marriage. Intimacy is not something we avoid because it is evil. It is something we wait for because it is good.

As for the honeymoon, many young couples might be consoled by the statement of Mark Twain that "on the typical honeymoon, the second biggest disappointment is the Niagara Falls." With tongue in cheek, the American humorist raised a serious question about a sensitive issue.

Many newly married couples are simply exhausted at the end of their wedding day, and a hectic wedding day may lead to a hectic wedding night. Both fatigue and emotional pressures do little to help sexual interaction.

Many newly married couples also begin a honeymoon with unrealistic expectations of what sexual fulfillment should be. In their recent text *Modern Marriage*,[9] Dr. Henry Bowman and Dr. Graham Spanier note many young couples expect to experience the equivalent of the San Francisco earthquake the first time they are intimate. If, as is usual, the experience is a shade milder, many head for the nearest technical manual to see what they are doing wrong. It takes time to develop full sexual adjustment. One cannot learn all there is to know in one short episode.

There may be a few awkward moments on the wedding night. This is particularly true if one of the partners, usually the husband, is in a hurry. Intimacy is never an emergency.

About sexuality in marriage, Dr. Bowman and Dr. Spanier observe:

In developing a new skill or new art, the novice makes many errors. In learning to walk, skate, play, swim, drive a golf ball, or bid a bridge hand, we perpetrate so many mistakes that after mastering the necessary, we look back in embarrassment at the immensity of previous ignorance, and the magnitude of our original awkwardness. We do not let our mistakes defeat us; nor stop with them.

A newly married couple, in many instances, is

confronted with the problem of learning a new art, acquiring a new skill. They are almost certain to make mistakes at first. They may feel that their ignorance is stupendous and their clumsiness colossal. They need not leap to conclusions and defeat themselves. They may learn by their mistakes. With patience, understanding, intelligence, self-analysis, an ample amount of love, and a liberal sprinkling of a sense of humor, errors may be corrected. Hence care, patience, perspective, and a will to succeed pay large dividends. (P. 259.)

While honeymoons may be disappointing for various reasons, most newly married couples report enjoying their honeymoons, even though problems may occur. And usually, as noted in the *Redbook* survey, sexual relations improve over a period of time. If dissatisfaction persists, a couple may want to seek help from their physician, their bishop, and a competent counselor. There are many resources to help couples achieve sexual fulfillment. Several helpful books are *Human Intimacy: Illusion and Reality* by Victor L. Brown, Jr. (Salt Lake City: Parliament Publishers, 1981); *And They Shall Be One Flesh* by Lindsay R. Curtis (Salt Lake City: Publishers Press, 1968); and *The Marriage Act: A Christian Guide to Sexual Love* by Tim and Beverly LeHaye (Grand Rapids: Zondervan Corporation, 1976).

Husband Too Busy

One of the advantages of writing a newspaper column about marriage is reading the letters received. It makes me aware of the concerns in contemporary marriages. Apparently, sexual adjustments are not limited to the early years of marriage, as indicated in the letter below.

Dear Dr. Barlow,
    My husband and I are in our early fifties and he is so involved in his occupation and church work that he is frequently away from home. This has created several

51

problems, one of which is that our children do not see him very much and I am raising them alone. But the most critical problem concerns me. He is so busy and gone so often that he seldom makes love to me. Sometimes we go for four or five weeks without any physical relationship at all. Is this normal? Could marital problems arise because of this trend?

My answer was:

To reply to your last question first, yes, serious problems could and often do arise in marriage when either or both of the marriage partners do not find sexual fulfillment in their relationship. This is particularly true if the lack of fulfillment occurs over months or years and resentment builds. With what is known about sexual relationships today, married people need not experience prolonged sexual frustration if both are willing to learn a few things and have a little patience with each other. Most married couples, I believe, can solve the vast majority of their marital problems alone, including sexual ones, if both husbands and wives are willing to cooperate with each other. On occasion, however, professional counseling or medical help may be sought if sincere effort has been made with little or no results.

As to your first question pertaining to the frequency of sexual relationships in marriage, allow me to make a few observations.

When it comes to making love, it has been noted that many people seem particularly preoccupied with numbers. In other words, how often is normal? Marriage counselors are frequently asked this question.

Several studies have been made that indicate the frequency of sexual relationships not only varies from couple to couple but also varies with the same couple from time to time. The length of time married, age, health status, resentment, guilt, the inability to communicate, particularly about sexual matters, all are factors. Immediate pressures such as business, emotional, social, family, and financial also seem to be variables which influence the frequency and intensity of physical intimacy in marriage.

Simply put, there is no set "normal frequency" pattern for sexual relationships. Most studies indicate that many married couples have sexual relations several times a month, so your pattern of once every four or five weeks is statistically atypical.

The most important factor, however, in sexual relationships in marriage is not so much with quantity, but with quality. Frequency is not nearly as important as satisfaction. Trying to bring satisfaction to your partner each time you do encounter lovemaking is far more important than trying to run a bedroom marathon. To find what brings satisfaction to each other in marriage suggests that a husband and wife must communicate about their sexual fulfillment, or lack of it. And when sexual frustration does occur, it should be dealt with quickly before a husband or wife becomes even more resentful.

If your sexual needs are not being met by your husband, you have every right in the world to tell him so. The tendency is for many married women to withhold this information and use it as a weapon in marriage or become the modern marriage martyr.

Once you tell him, let's assume that he will arrange to stay home more with you and your family. Perhaps he will try to meet your needs a little more, rather than give way to the many occupational obligations of his job or demands of his church.

In my humble opinion, any husband too busy to make love is simply too busy.

The Three Rs of Infidelity

There are additional potential problems if a husband and wife go for prolonged periods of time without sexual relationships. It sometimes leads to infidelity. When a couple marries, it is implied in the wedding vows that they will "forsake all others." Within the Church, of course, it is explicit that this means forgoing any sexual relationship with any other person.

The question has recently arisen as to how many married people actually live up to this vow. Whatever the trends and statistics may be, enough married people are unfaithful to raise another interesting question: How do couples who originally commit themselves to forsake all others become sexually involved with other people?

In his book *Couples*,[10] Dr. Carlfred Broderick, marriage counselor from the University of Southern California, notes, "Over the years I have listened to the explanations of dozens of individuals who, despite such a commitment [of fidelity], found themselves involved in adulterous relationships. Again and again, their stories revolved around three issues which I have come to think of as the three R's of infidelity: Resentment, Rationalization and Rendezvous." (P. 161.)

Resentment. Dr. Broderick reports that most unfaithful married people resent their spouses. Usually, they have not found a way to deal with marital problems or resentments. Dr. Broderick notes that the preventative for infidelity "is a developed and well-oiled mechanism for dealing with strain in the marriage."

Another frequent source of resentment in marriage comes from sexuality, and too often people enter marriage with unrealistic expectations about it. When the expectations go unfulfilled over a long time, resentment builds. Then people sometimes seek a new relationship to find what they feel is lacking in the present one.

Rationalization. If a married person becomes unfaithful, he or she uses some degree of rationalization. The person may simply deny the possibility of getting involved with someone else. A wife may flirt with another man and yet feel it means nothing. Or a husband may be high on drugs or alcohol, become uninhibited, and deny that anything will or could happen, when it already is occurring.

But, Dr. Broderick reports, the most interesting form of rationalization involves virtue rather than vice. He notes, "I am convinced that more people get themselves into the pain of infidelity through empathy, concern and compassion than through a base motive. . . . With a little help from rationalization, sympathy leads smoothly into tenderness, the tenderness to the need for privacy, the privacy to physical consolation, and the consolation straight to bed." (P. 163.)

Rendezvous. A rendezvous is a meeting or an appointment to meet, and infidelity depends on a rendezvous if it is to occur. But Dr. Broderick suggests there are some intermediate steps.

Most extramarital relationships begin, interestingly enough, as friendships and "just happen." Two people meet at unplanned places such as work, parties, or the like. From these unstructured meetings they proceed to systematic associations that appear to be legitimate. There are more frequent meetings at work or parties. Husbands and company secretaries find excuses to be together for lunch "for business reasons," or two neighbors find their friendship escalating and one finally invites the other over when the spouse is gone.

A house guest sometimes turns into a sexual host, or a wife and a fellow male student may find they have more in common than a college course. A husband and a female co-worker find they spend hours planning together, but their planning eventually goes beyond their jobs.

From these systematic associations, couples plan for and seek a private or secret rendezvous so often associated with infidelity. And that is usually when it occurs. Dr. Broderick concludes, "If you find yourself in a situation involving a delicious privacy with an attractive member of the opposite sex, you should begin to look for ways to restructure the situation. No doubt you will think of a dozen reasons why it is unreasonable to go out of your way to avoid perfectly legitimate and innocent companionship, but then that may simply mean you need to review the three R's of infidelity one more time." (P. 166.)

Never Too Old

Undoubtedly there are also sexual adjustments during the later years of marriage. But it is becoming increasingly evident that many of those problems are culturally induced. An undergraduate class at Brandeis University was asked to complete the following: "Sex for most old people is _____ ." What would you have written if given the same assignment?

Perhaps your answers would be similar to those of the Brandeis students who stated that sex for most old people is "unimportant," "past," "negligible," "nonexistent," and so on. Sexual functioning, however, depends to a great extent on one's attitudes and beliefs, and for many people the expectation that sex is nonexistent in the later years of married life may become a self-fulfilling prophecy. Others, who reach the age of sixty-five and find that they still have strong sexual desires, may be overcome with guilt and erroneously believe they are "oversexed."

Sexuality for the elderly is not a recent invention. It has been important to most elderly people who have been studied. Sexuality is not just the ability to have sexual intercourse; for many it is the need for continued closeness, affection, intimacy, and romance.

With our recent acquisition of knowledge about human behavior, we have become aware of several contemporary needs. We need to recognize the normalcy of sexuality. We also need to clear away the obstacles in people's minds that prevent the expression of affection and intimacy in the later years.

In his book *Sexual Life After Sixty*,[11] Dr. Isadore Rubin lists some of the prevalent myths many people, including some of the elderly, have about sexuality. Three of those myths are the vital fluids myth, the menopause myth, and the hysterectomy myth.

The vital fluids myth, according to Dr. Rubin, is the belief that sexual intercourse weakens a person, since semen is deemed to be one of the vital fluids of the body. "It is a major self-defeating myth," the author notes, "which discourages sexuality in the older years." The corollary of this belief is that if one abstains from intimacy during the later years of life and thereby retains this vital body fluid, the catastrophe of old age will be avoided and life prolonged. Even more specific, according to Dr. Rubin, is the common belief that each drop of semen emitted is equal to the loss of forty drops of blood. "Such myths die very hard," he notes, "particularly if they are constantly repeated by what often seem to be scientific sources."

Still another major misconception is the belief that menopause means the end of a woman's sexuality. This is particularly true when reproduction is thought to be the only purpose of sex. Many believe that if a woman is no longer capable of having children, she no longer needs sexual interaction. Dr. Rubin reports that as late as 1931, one medical authority defined menopause as "that time in a woman's life at which her sexual activities come to their natural termination," asserting that "the cessation of the monthly recurring menstrual flow indicates that the termination of sexual activity has arrived." The same medical doctor could not account, however, for the common-sense observation that the sexual desire not only continues in many women after menopause, but for some actually increases.

A third major myth has to do with hysterectomy, the partial or complete removal of the uterus. A hysterectomy does not create any physical inability that would prevent either the husband or wife from attaining sexual satisfaction, except in very rare cases. What a hysterectomy may change, according to Dr. Rubin, is the husband's or wife's mental attitude and their expectations of what will now happen in their sexual relationship. Unfortunately, mental changes can be as effective as physical changes in ending sexual fulfillment.

Enough studies have been conducted to lay aside the myths about menopause and hysterectomies. If the sex life deteriorates seriously after either of these two events, the cause should be sought not so much in the physical but in the psychological aspect of the couple's relationship.

The sexual relationship today is being more and more recognized as a rich and vital aspect of human relationships. It is another language by which couples share deep intimacies. The importance of sexuality has been recognized for younger married couples, but it has certainly not yet been widely advocated for older married people. Preoccupation with the security needs of the aged has led most people to overlook their sexual needs altogether. Not until recently have we been made aware of the importance of sex to the psychological well-being of older married persons in our society as well as the young.

There is little doubt that the sexual lives of elderly couples can be far richer than most people realize. As Martin Berezin of Harvard University explained, "The one thing which neither grows old nor diminishes is the need for love and affection. These drives, these wishes never change." In essence, you are never too old.

Some Thoughts on Having Children

Another letter I received had to do with sexual intimacy and controlling conception. A husband wrote:

Dear Dr. Barlow,

I have enjoyed reading your column for over a year and read what you wrote concerning hormones and moodiness in women and would be interested in your thoughts on what our doctor calls "Tired Wife Syndrome."

My wife had a physical checkup and the doctor gave her a prescription for a drug. He told her that it wasn't hormones or a chemical imbalance that was causing her to feel depressed or be out of patience with the children. He said it was just a case of tired wife syndrome caused mainly by having children too fast and no energy to cope.

We decided after our third child was born marking three of our four years of marriage, that we needed to wait for an indefinite period of time before having another child. This brings up another question. What are your feelings on controlling conception? We would appreciate your thoughts on this area.

My answer was:

Married couples, and particularly newlyweds, face both opportunities and challenges in contemporary marriage. And many of those opportunities and challenges are in the realm of having children. How many? How far in between? And, when to begin?

Students in my marriage classes have frequently asked such questions. Here are some of the guidelines I have suggested:

1. Children should be perceived as a source of fulfillment and growth rather than as a source of stagnation and confinement.

2. A couple will likely find joy in parenthood if they have as many children as they desire and can care for.

3. Many couples use discretion when to have a second, third, or an additional child. That same wisdom and discretion can and ought to be used to decide when to have the first child.

4. How many children a couple will have, and when, are decisions that only the couple, with the guidance of their Father in heaven, can make, since they are the ones who must experience the consequences of their decisions.

5. Almost every married couple will confront the situation of controlling conception. And most couples, by one means or another, will choose to control conception during some part of their marriage. Otherwise, each couple could have nearly twenty children. The inability or unwillingness to decide about controlling conception is, in essence, a decision to have a child.

6. If, for certain personal reasons, a couple decides that having a child, or another child, immediately is unwise, the choice of method is one that each could and should decide in consultation with their physician and in the context of their religious beliefs. Methods vary in reliability and each has its own advantages and disadvantages. Abstinence is one way to control conception. Like any other method, abstinence has side effects, some of which are harmful to the marriage relationship. Also, I believe abortion is not an acceptable way to control conception.

7. Since the woman has the greater responsibility not only of bearing children but also in caring for and rearing them during their childhood, her physical and emotional health should be a major consideration in making decisions about having children.

8. Decisions about controlling conception will vary from couple to couple. What may be appropriate for one couple may be inappropriate for another. We should, therefore, not judge others' decisions.

9. Having children involves more than physically bearing them. Parents are to provide for the physical, emotional, and social well-being of their children and teach them moral values. Having children and failing to provide these things could have serious implications for both parents and children.

10. The sexual relationship has several functions, two of which are reproduction and relationship enhancement. When conception is not desired or no longer possible, it does not mean that sexual relationships should cease.

11. Married couples ought to examine their motives for having children. We should have children not just because of social or peer pressure, but because we genuinely want them. Guilt is a questionable incentive for having children.

Since controlling conception is a concern for many Latter-day Saint couples, the following may be informative.

Dr. Homer Ellsworth, a gynecologist and former member of the Melchizedek Priesthood General Committee was asked, "Is it our understanding that we are to propagate children as long and as frequently as the human body will permit? Is there not any kind of 'gospel family-planning,' for lack of a better way to say it?"

Dr. Ellsworth's comments were printed in the August 1979 *Ensign*, pages 23-24. Following are some of his thoughts in answering the question:

I hear this type of question frequently from active and committed Latter-day Saints who often ask questions that are outside my professional responsibilities. Here are some of the principles and attitudes I believe apply to this fundamental question, a question most couples ask themselves many times during their child-bearing years.

I rejoice in our basic understanding of the plan of salvation, which teaches us that we come to earth for growth and maturity, and for testing. In that process we may marry and provide temporal bodies for our Heavenly Father's spirit children. That's basic, it seems to me. In contemplating this truth, I also take great delight in the Church's affirmative position that it is our blessing and joy, and our spiritual obligation, to bear children and to have a family. It impresses me that the positive is stressed as our goal.

I rejoice in our understanding that one of the most fundamental principles in the plan of salvation is free agency. The opportunity to make free agency choices is so important that our Heavenly Father was willing to withhold additional opportunities from a third of his children rather than deprive them of their right of choice. This principle of free agency is vital to the success of our probation. Many of the decisions we make involve the application of principles where precise yes-and-no answers are just not available in Church handbooks, meetings, or even the scriptures.

Our growth process, then, results from weighing the alternatives, studying the matter carefully, and seeking inspiration from the Lord. This, it seems to me, is at the heart of the gospel plan. It has always given me great joy and confidence to observe that in their administration of God's teachings, our inspired prophets do not seek to violate this general plan of individual agency, but operate within broad guidelines that provide considerable individual flexibility.

I recall a President of the Church, now deceased, who visited his daughter in the hospital following a miscarriage.

She was the mother of eight children and was in her early forties. She asked, "Father, may I quit now?" His response was, "Don't ask me. That decision is between you, your husband, and your Father in Heaven. If you two can face him with a good conscience and can say you have done the best you could, that you have really tried, then you may quit. But, that is between you and him. I have enough problems of my own to talk over with him when we meet!" So it is clear to me that the decisions regarding our children, when to have them, their number, and all related matters and questions can only be made after real discussion between the marriage partners and after prayer.

In this process of learning what is right for you at any particular time, I have always found it helpful to use a basic measuring stick: *Is it selfish?* I have concluded that most of our sins are really sins of selfishness. If you don't pay your tithing selfishness is at the heart of it. If you commit adultery, selfishness is at the heart of it. If you are dishonest, selfishness is at the heart of it. I have noted that many times in the scriptures we observe the Lord chastising people because of their selfishness. Thus, on the family questions, if we limit our families because we are self-centered or materialistic, we will surely develop a character based on selfishness. As the scriptures make clear, that is not a description of a celestial character. I have found that we really have to analyze ourselves to discover our motives. Sometimes superficial motivations and excuses show up when we do that.

But, on the other hand, we need not be afraid of studying the question from important angles—the physical or mental health of the mother and father, the parents' capacity to provide basic necessities, and so on. If for certain personal reasons a couple prayerfully decides that having another child immediately is unwise, the method of spacing children—discounting possible medical or physical effects—makes little difference. Abstinence, of course, is also a form of contraception, and like any other method it has side effects, some of which are harmful to the marriage relationship.

As a physician I am often required to treat social-emotional symptoms related to various aspects of living. In doing so I have always been impressed that our prophets past and present have never stipulated that bearing children was the sole function of the marriage relationship. Prophets have taught that physical intimacy is a strong force in strengthening the love bond in marriage, enhancing and reinforcing marital unity. Indeed, it is the rightful gift of God to the married. . . .

So, as to the number and spacing of children, and other related questions on this subject, such decisions are to be made by husband and wife righteously and empathetically communicating together and seeking the inspiration of the Lord. I believe that the prophets have given wise counsel when they advise couples to be considerate and plan carefully so that the mother's health will not be impaired. When this recommendation of the First Presidency is ignored or unknown or misinterpreted, heartache can result.

As I meet other people and learn of their circumstances, I am continually inspired by the counsel of the First Presidency in the *General Handbook of Instructions* that the health of the mother and the well-being of the family should be considered. Thirty-four years as a practicing gynecologist and as an observer of Latter-day Saint families have taught me that not only the physical well-being but the emotional well-being must also be considered. Some parents are less subject to mood swings and depression and can more easily cope with the pressures of many children. Some parents have more help from their families and friends. Some are more effective parents than others, even when their desire and motivation are the same. In addition, parents do owe their children the necessities of life. The desire for luxuries, of course, would not be an appropriate determinant of family size; luxuries are just not a legitimate consideration. I think every inspired human heart can quickly determine what is luxury and what is not.

In summary, it is clear to me that couples not let the things that matter most be at the mercy of those that matter least. In searching for what is most important, I believe that we are accountable not only for what we do but for why we do it. Thus, regarding family size, spacing of children, and attendant questions, we should desire to multiply and replenish the earth as the Lord commands us. In that process, Heavenly Father intends that we use the free agency he has given in charting a wise course for ourselves and our families. We gain the wisdom to chart that wise course through study, prayer, and listening to the still small voice within us.

4

FATHERHOOD

Martin Luther once said, "No man is so virtuous as to marry a wife only to have children." *Having* children is obviously a joint venture between husband and wife even though the father's part is minimal in comparison to that of the mother. And, as far as *rearing* children in America, the same trend seems evident. After the children are born, fathers often have little, if anything, to do with their rearing. This was apparent in numerous letters I received and in the survey. Of the twenty items in the profile, the one on helping rear and discipline the children was ranked fourth.

During the last decade there have been some interesting discussions about single-parent families, which now constitute some eleven percent of all families in the United States. Approximately ninety percent of single-parent families, incidently, are headed by women. The question has been raised whether or not one parent can adequately raise a family. The pros and cons are weighed and the debate continues. But it also has been noted that in intact, two-parent families, most children are reared by the mother anyway. In America, we are almost to the point where parenthood means motherhood. The wives who wrote me letters and responded to my questionnaires want help from their husbands in rearing their children. They wrote:

"I love our children dearly and have enjoyed being a mother. I have been able to accept my husband's lifestyle most of the time even though it has not always been easy. It is apparent now that I probably should have insisted that he spend more time being a father and husband. Our children would have benefited from a closer relationship with their father. He is a very wise, brilliant man, and is sensitive and caring with others, particularly in his church work. But he is unable to respond to his children in this same manner. He has felt his responsibility so keenly, I guess, that he becomes the authoritarian father and lectures instead of discussing. Well, it just didn't seem worth the hassle and unpleasantness to attempt to show him how much we need and want part of him and some of the charm that he shows so abundantly to others."

"I wish my husband would take the time to listen and understand the needs of each child, the younger ones as well as the older ones. I would like him to have the kind of relationship with his children that he has with me. Then we could share our thoughts on how to fulfill the needs of each child and demonstrate our love for them as my husband and I try to do for each other."

"I wish my husband would spend more time with the children and help them with their chores, homework and getting ready for bed. And I wish he would do it willingly instead of hollering at them all the time. It is hard for me to keep up with all the children and follow through on each task alone."

"I want my husband to read bedtime stories to our children and in general make more effort to play with them, talk to them, and do things with them. I would appreciate it if he would encourage them to obey and help me. And if they see their Daddy helping clear the table and keep the clothes and rooms picked up, I feel they would respond better."

Apparently some fathers are involving themselves more with rearing the children, as was expressed in some of the letters. Some appreciative wives wrote:

"Whenever my husband is home in the evening he puts our three children to bed. This is the time the children spend with their father, talking together while they prepare for bed and say their prayers. It has made each of the children feel closer to their father. I appreciate the break it gives me from the children, and they respond so much better to him after having listened to me most of the day. It also gives me a chance to clean the kitchen and straighten the house before going to bed."

"My husband is a full partner in parenting. Although I am with the children all day while he is at work, he talks to me during the day about their activities, progress, and needs. When he comes home, he plays with them and takes care of them while I prepare dinner. He helps get them to bed and gets up with them in the night as often as I do."

"My husband shares his time with the children. Rearing children is a joint project, never Dad with the football game and Mom with the kids. He also supports what I say when disciplining the children, by saying 'Do what your mother says!' and then if there is ever a question, my husband and I discuss it privately at another time."

Children and Marriage

In his book *Marriage Happiness*[1], David Knox states that children are inextricably involved in the marital relationship. A couple recently told me that if they did not have their children, they would have few marital problems. Such a statement is an oversimplification, but it bears a thread of truth. (A friend

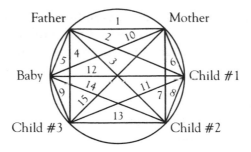

Before the baby arrived, there were ten relationships in the family, but when the baby was born, each family member had a new relationship, adding not one, but five, relationships to the family for a new total of fifteen. So we see the complexity of the family change as each child is born and additional demands are made on mother.

It is little wonder that with each new baby a wife needs and wants more help from her husband in rearing the children. A mother of ten children said, "The more children we have, the less help I get." How many relationships are in her family of twelve (two parents and ten children)? Use the formula to find out. Is it any wonder she would like some help from her husband? Between husband, wife, and children, she has *sixty-six* relationships to monitor. But in her case, the help from husband decreased as the family complexity increased.

A Wife's Major Satisfactions

Of all the relationships in a family, which one is the most crucial? In families where both parents are present, it is always the one between husband and wife. Why? Because when that relationship is threatened, or impaired, it influences all other relationships in the family. When we talk about having strong family ties, we often think of the parent-child relationship. But the most important part of family life is marriage.

Sometimes we become so preoccupied with being good parents that we neglect our spouses. And by so doing, we undermine our capabilities as fathers and mothers. Dr. Larry Hof and Dr. William Miller, marriage counselors and educators

70

from Philadelphia, have recently written *Marriage Enrichment, Philosophy, Process and Program.*[2] In it, they note: "This book focuses almost exclusively on marriage enrichment because of our belief that the most effective and efficient way to enrich families is to focus on the husband-wife relationship. We believe the quality of the marriage greatly influences, and may in fact determine, the quality of the total family relationship. This does not negate the value of looking upon the family as an integrated system, but rather emphasizes the central importance of the marital dyad in the larger system of the family." (P. 3.)

Dr. Hof and Dr. Miller raise an interesting point. When both a father and mother are in the home, can we have strong family ties without first having strong marital relationships?

While attending college several years ago, my dorm mother was Jean May. We called her Sister May. She was nearly seventy years old. One evening she invited a few of us into her apartment for doughnuts, and we began talking, of all things, about marriage and family. The conversation lasted late into the evening, and toward the end of our get-together, she asked a question I have never forgotten: "Where do you think most women get their major satisfactions in life?" she asked. "From their husbands or from their children?"

We talked it over for a few minutes, and as single, young men unanimously agreed that most women derive their major satisfactions and fulfillment from their husbands.

Sister May rocked a few times in her rocking chair and said, "I think I disagree. I have observed that most women get it from their children." She nibbled on her doughnut and continued, "It's not that women want it that way. Fulfillment is often sought in children because it is all too often missing with husbands."

She made that comment nearly twenty years ago, and I haven't been able to get it out of my mind. Is parental fulfillment often sought by husband and wife because of marital dissatisfaction? And need it be?

One thing for certain, children leave home sooner or later. Where does that leave Mom and Dad? All too often, they find themselves living with a stranger who, over the years, served as a partner in parenting.

In summary, Dr. Hof and Dr. Miller believe that the quality of the marital relationship greatly influences the quality of the total family relationship. If they are correct, perhaps we husbands should give greater attention to our wives in order to strengthen our families.

The Courage to Be Imperfect

While most men are not giving enough time and attention to being a father, a few go to the other extreme and become preoccupied with the role. A father may worry how his children compare to those of his neighbors and friends. Or he may compare himself to other fathers and then worry and fret because he does not seem to have the same skills and attitudes as other fathers.

It may be that his excessive self-consciousness as a father actually hinders him in his role. Being an effective father does require persistent effort and thought. But even in the best of families, mistakes are going to be made by fathers, mothers, and children. Positive outcomes in rearing children do not always come about as a result of following a formula. Children will mature and grow, hopefully with the help of, but sometimes in spite of, their parents.

Perhaps we fathers, particularly new ones, might relax a little more with our children. We could make a concerted effort to rear them adequately, but also learn to enjoy them. And in the process, we could allow for some mistakes to occur. President Brigham Young said, "We are not required in our sphere to be as perfect as Gods and angels are in their spheres." (*Journal of Discourses* 10:223.) President Young also said, "Those who do right, and seek the glory of the Father in heaven, whether their knowledge be little or much, or whether they can do little, or much, if they do the very best they know how, they are perfect. . . . When we are doing as well as we know how in the sphere, and station which we occupy here . . . we are justified." (Deseret News, August 31, 1854, p. 1.)

Dr. Rudolf Dreikurs notes in his book *Children: The Challenge*[3], "Parental perfection is an impossible goal, and striving for it seldom leads to improvement, but more often to giving up in despair. We all make mistakes. Very few are disastrous. Many times we won't even know that a given action is a mistake until after it is done and we see the results! Sometimes we even have to make the mistake in order to find out that it is a mistake. *We must have the courage to be imperfect* and allow our children also to be imperfect. Only in this way can we function, progress, and grow." (P. 108; italics added.)

Father Types

Whether or not they realize it, most fathers have a model for interacting with their children. In his book *Parents in Modern America*,[4] E. E. LeMasters describes five such models and notes the advantages and disadvantages of each. The five models (relevant for mothers as well) are (1) father as martyr; (2) father as buddy or pal; (3) father as policeman or drill sergeant; (4) father as teacher-counselor; and (5) father as coach. Let us briefly examine each.

Father as martyr. Many fathers, without knowing it, adopt the martyr model, wanting only the best for their children. They are willing to sacrifice almost anything, including themselves, for the benefit of their children. Martyr fathers say such things as "Nothing is too good for my children" or "I would do anything for my child." While this appears to be a virtuous attitude, the martyr father does not often act in the best interests of either himself or his children.

Altruism is a desirable part of family life. But if the giving and caring is one sided, as it often is with martyr fathers, the one giving is often taken advantage of by the one receiving.

Martyr fathers usually feel guilty because they are not doing enough for their children. Nor will they ever be able to do so. Having taught at five universities in the United States, I have often been amazed at the hostility and resentment many students have for their parents. I realized that many of these students were coddled and pampered as children. They were

73

usually given gifts and many material things, along with an excess of attention, which is equally detrimental to a child's well-being. Many children of martyr fathers (and mothers) expect their parents to continue to give after they leave home. When the parents can no longer maintain the level of giving, the children are often offended and question the love of the parent.

Most martyr fathers overprotect their children, since they feel excessively responsible and guilt-ridden in their role as parent. Neither guilt nor overprotection is conducive to the well-being of parent or child, particularly as the child matures. Dependent children eventually become demanding children.

The child of a martyr father or mother will almost always revolt and reach out for a more flexible life-style both in and outside the home as he learns to be an individual. Such revolt usually brings conflict with the martyr parent, who then takes the attitude, "Look what you're doing to me—and after all I've done for you." Such words, often uttered as the martyr parent ages, only bring frustration and guilt upon the child.

Father as buddy or pal. Many fathers, particularly those of the middle-class, have adopted the role model of a buddy or pal. Fathers are supposed to play ball with their children, play games with them, and "get down on their level." While fathers need to play and spend time with children, there are some problems with the "buddy-pal" model of fathering.

Many fathers try the buddy role as a last resort. "If you can't beat 'em, join 'em." The father tries to join his child's peer group, much as a social worker infiltrates juvenile street gangs in large cities. As social workers seek acceptance and try to influence the gang leadership, they operate on one other premise: they have no authority in the gang! Such a role is not only difficult but dangerous for a father to assume.

Sensing that many youth mistrust older people, fathers will often seek the pal or buddy model to alleviate this mistrust. Many people generally do not revere the aged, and some even tend to pity them. And children soon incorporate these values. Since we tend to dichotomize people into being either young or old, many fathers (and mothers) disassociate themselves from the old group and try to involve themselves with the young.

In many ways, the buddy model is extremely unrealistic. If being a pal means being "equal" to a child emotionally and intellectually, the child is free to receive or reject any advice from his father just as he would from any other friend. By law, parents are responsible to rear and guide their children. But letting a child arbitrarily accept or reject parental guidance is demeaning for the parent. This model may work well for very young parents of very young children or teenagers, and it may work well for parents during recreation with their children. But when it comes to the "shoulds" and "should nots," to "yes" and "no," a father-as-buddy will lose much of his influence over the child. Rather than trying to act like and be accepted by youth, parents should act their age, whatever it may be.

The buddy role also involves considerable risk, since there is a tendency to retreat to a more formal, authoritarian model if things do not go well. This shift in role model is difficult for a father to manage without damaging his image in the eyes of the child. In other words, the "friendship" is threatened and may even cease when the "pal" becomes authoritarian.

Father as policeman or drill sergeant. This is the traditional authoritarian father who sees his responsibility as making sure his children understand various rules and then punishing the children for disobedience. Such fathers believe this model will keep children from getting into trouble. If they do get into trouble, the father can always defend himself by saying, "I told him not to do it."

This role is not always effective, particularly in a society becoming more democratic and advocating social equality. Just because an adult tells someone younger to do something does not necessarily mean it will be done. Excellent reviews of rearing children in a society advocating social equality are *Social Equality: The Challenge of Today*[5] and *Children: The Challenge*[6], both written by Dr. Rudolf Dreikurs. In the latter book, he notes:

> Rapid changes take place, but few are aware of the nature of the changes. It is largely the impact of democ-

racy that has transformed our social atmosphere and made the traditional methods of child-raising obsolete. We no longer have rules such as prevailed in the autocratic society from which we are emerging. In a society of equals we can't rule over another. Equality means that each decides for himself. In an autocratic society, the ruler was superior to and had the power over the submissive. Regardless of his station in the world, the father of each family ruled over the members, including the wife. Today, this is no longer true. Women proclaimed their equality with men; and as the husband lost his power over his wife, both parents lost their power over their children. This was the beginning of the general social upheaval that has been widely felt but little understood. (P. 7.)

While the policeman model may work while the children are young, it rarely functions as the child matures. The father will have to abandon his badge and swagger stick about the time of the pre-teens if he wants to maintain any reasonable rapport with his children, particularly after they leave home.

The policeman model may work for some fathers who can convey a great deal of love simultaneously with strict discipline. They can become benevolent despots. But relatively few fathers who adopt this model have either the love or the capacity to convey love to the subordinated child.

Father as teacher-counselor. Like the previous models, this one has some advantages in that fathers and mothers do have things they want to teach their children. This is particularly true in the area of moral or spiritual values.

The teacher-counselor father assumes that the child has almost unlimited potential for growth, and that the role of the parent is to tap that potential. This model is also based on the assumption that the father knows all the right answers. The only problem, supposedly, is to motivate the child to find out what the right answers are.

Within the middle class, this is the dominant model. While it has some fine features, it also creates some problems. This model is excessively child oriented. Since children are supposedly very teachable, the father feels responsible to make his children "into something." Their success or failure, according to this model, depends on the skills of the father. And since the child is the center of the father's universe, he or she often receives excessive attention and becomes spoiled. But little attention is given to the needs of the father or the needs of society in this way of rearing children. And since the father is never sure how his children will turn out he often feels guilty if they do not follow his teachings.

Father as coach. Perhaps the father-as-coach model is better than the preceding models. At some point children must leave home, and yet parents want them to retain some relationship with them during and after their presence in the home. How might parents accomplish this?

First of all, they would see their role as parents beyond the immediacy of day-to-day living. Physically, most children will leave home around their eighteenth year. Psychologically, however, children begin to separate themselves from father and mother as they enter the teens. And maybe what parents can do best is to prepare them to leave home and live in the larger world.

With this perspective, everything we do should prepare our children to function separately, autonomously, and happily in society. The home becomes a microcosm of the larger world, a mini-world where we train children to cope outside the home. The childhood threats of "leaving home" are a prototype of what is to come. Knowing that one day our children will leave, we loosen our grip on them gradually so the transition is not abrupt.

In our home, then, we are going to coach our children in the strategies of life's "game." We are going to teach them the skills for daily living and then hold frequent practice sessions in the home. We will learn together to deal with such things as love, forgiveness, sharing, anger, lying, cheating, and confrontation, and try to understand these behaviors and their consequences.

We will have to be aware of our children's fitness (physical, mental, moral, and spiritual) and have some knowledge of the arena in which they are going to play. We will be aware of both old and new rules. Children must develop stamina, assertiveness, and a competitive spirit. And they must accept some rules of discipline.

We will teach our children that they must sometimes subordinate self for the success of the team. In addition, we will always have the welfare of our players in mind. And most important, we will remember that once the game is underway, it is up to the players to win or lose. The coach must stand on the sidelines and see the results of long and strenuous practice games, of chalk-talks, simulated plays, and constant critiquing of skills and knowledge in scrimmage sessions. But once the players are on the field, they assume the responsibility for the outcome, win or lose. They must strive not only to win but also learn to live with defeat.

Like the other four models, this one has limitations. A coach often has professional preparation, while a father has little other than what he learned from his father. A coach can select his players, but a father must prepare and play everyone in every game, regardless of talent. In difficult situations, coaches can substitute. Fathers cannot. A coach can see the immediate results of his efforts. A father has to wait thirty or forty years to see the final results of his efforts. Coaches can quit or get fired. Parents usually can't. And coaches are expected to at least respect their players, regardless of performance. Parents, however, are expected to love their children, no matter what.

All these are just models, and have only limited application to fatherhood. We don't want to make fatherhood overly complicated. If we don't become obsessed with the role, if we learn to help our wives, we will probably do adequately.

Bows, Strings, and Arrows

All people, husbands, wives, and children, are unique individuals but have chosen to become involved in relationships that require some cooperation and identification with others. The most intimate of these is marriage. The most encompassing is family. How might a proper balance be struck in all these responsibilities?

I like the analogy of Cyril Connolly. He says the perfect union between man and woman is like a strung bow. Who is to say whether the string bends the bow or the bow tightens the string? Yet male bow and female string are in harmony with each other, and their arrow can be aimed. Too taut, the bow or string will break. Unstrung, the bow hangs aimless; the cord flaps idly.

In *The Prophet*, Kahlil Gibran compares marriage and parenthood with the bow, and children with arrows:

> Your children are not your children.
> They are the sons and daughters of Life's longing
>   for itself.
> They come through you but not from you,
> And though they are with you yet they belong
>   not to you.
>
> You may give them your love but not your thoughts,
> For they have their own thoughts.
> You may house their bodies but not their souls,
> For their souls dwell in the house of tomorrow,
>   which you cannot visit, not even in your dreams.
> You may strive to be like them, but seek not to make
>   them like you.
> For life goes not backward nor tarries with yesterday.
>
> You are the bows from which your children as
>   living arrows are sent forth.
> The archer sees the mark upon the path of the infinite,
>   and He bends you with His might that His arrows
>   may go swift and far.
> Let your bending in the archer's hand be for gladness;
> For even as He loves the arrow that flies, so He loves
>   also the bow that is stable.[7]

5

SPIRITUALITY

One of the interesting findings of the "Profile of a Loving Husband" was that the item "He helps me attain my spiritual needs" was ranked fifth out of twenty items. The conclusion could be made that the respondents to the survey were mainly from the intermountain area where religion, particularly the Latter-day Saint religion, is a dominant part of life. But it is likely that having spiritual needs fulfilled in marriage is important for other wives as well.

According to my letters, conversations, and survey results, a husband may give gifts, do many deeds to convey love, learn to communicate, help with the children, and do many other things conducive to a successful marriage. But until he learns to help his wife meet her spiritual needs, they both may never find the fulfillment possible in their marriage.

Here are some comments of wives about spiritual matters in marriage:

> "Something I would like to do with my husband in the future is to spend more time growing together spiritually. I can have a spiritual experience by myself, but it is so much better if we can share that time and experience together. Whenever I am close to my Heavenly Father I feel close to my husband also, and if he is with

me, at my side, it makes me feel much closer to God. The best way for us to increase our love for each other is to have many spiritual experiences together."

"My husband could show his love to me in the future by continuing to put the Lord first in his life and also letting me know he loves me in his daily acts and words."

"I need example, the example of a husband who is striving to attain the same spiritual goals as I am. Also, I need encouragement from my husband to do the things I believe I should do."

"I need a husband who will be the spiritual leader in our home. I need to be able to depend on him to seek the guidance of the Lord concerning our family."

"My husband helps me find the time each day, without interruptions from the children, so I can read, study, meditate, and pray. (Of course I should do the same for him.)"

"I wish my husband would initiate family discussions on spiritual matters. I guess he thinks I am the leader of the children and expects me to follow through with their prayers, etc."

"I need my husband to set an example of the basic Christian teachings, such as total honesty to everyone, keeping the Sabbath day holy, etc."

"My husband loves me enough to take me to church frequently."

"My husband could be more consistent and take more responsibility for having family prayers and spiritual talks with our children. It would greatly increase the spirituality in our home."

"My husband and I try to pray together frequently. It starts our day off right."

"My husband and I enjoy attending our Church and taking part in it. We try and support each other in our church work."

"Since becoming parents, we have found prayer to be an important part of our lives."

"As a wife I have a need not only to understand the scriptures, but also a need to discuss them with someone. My husband reads and discusses the scriptures with me often."

When Susan and I were attending graduate school at Florida State University, we met another couple, Scott and Beverly Zimmerman, with whom we have retained a friendship for many years. We have always felt that Scott and Beverly were deeply committed Latter-day Saints. After graduating from Florida State, we and the Zimmermans lived in different parts of the United States while teaching at various universities and now, ten years later, we find ourselves living in the same neighborhood and attending the same ward.

A few weeks ago, Beverly and I were in the chapel foyer with our small children during sacrament meeting (it's called the First Church of the Foyer). I was explaining to Beverly my interest that spirituality ranked so high in the "Profile of a Loving Husband." Knowing Beverly's interest in the matter, I asked her how she felt a husband could help his wife attain her spiritual needs. She responded with the following ideas:

A husband can help his wife fulfill her spiritual needs by supporting her efforts to reach her spiritual goals. Business partners realize that a strong company depends on the success of both partners. A married couple likewise must realize that a strong marriage depends on the success of both the husband and wife. A husband who supports his wife in achieving her spiritual goals will see the whole marriage benefit.

A married couple needs to be able to discuss their individual and joint spiritual goals and how they can help each other achieve these goals. For example, the wife may have an individual goal to study the scriptures but never seems to find time during a busy day of caring for several small children. The husband might agree to put the children to bed one night a week to give his wife an evening of uninterrupted study. Or the wife may have a goal of providing compassionate service to her neighbors. She decides to send a warm meal to a sick neighbor's home. Her husband might support her by not complaining if his own meal needs to be rewarmed. The couple should have a joint goal of teaching moral principles to their children. The husband can support that goal by having family discussions about it.

A husband can help his wife spiritually by treating her as his spiritual peer. He can share his personal experiences and spiritual insights with his wife and seek her advice on scriptural matters. He should realize that a woman's spiritual well-being is closely related to her physical and emotional well-being and make sure her needs in these areas are being met as well.

A Spiritual Leader Speaks

President Spencer W. Kimball, in his book *Marriage*,[1] states:

> There is a never-failing formula that will guarantee to every couple a happy and eternal marriage; but like all formulas, the principle ingredients must not be left out, reduced, nor limited. . . . The formula is simple; the ingredients are few, though there are many amplifications of each.
>
> First, there must be the proper approach toward marriage, which contemplates the selection of a spouse

83

who reaches as nearly as possible the pinnacle of perfection in all the matters that are of importance to the individuals. Then those two parties must come to the altar in the temple realizing that they must work hard toward this successful joint living.

Second, there must be great unselfishness, forgetting self and directing all of the family life and all pertaining thereunto to the good of the family, and subjugating self.

Third, there must be continued courting and expressions of affection, kindness, and consideration to keep love alive and growing.

Fourth, there must be complete living of the commandments of the Lord as defined in the gospel of Jesus Christ.

With these ingredients properly mixed and continually kept functioning, it is quite impossible for unhappiness to come, for misunderstandings to continue, or for breaks to occur.

Defining Spirituality

It is generally understood that spirituality is a rather subjective area of marriage. Many husbands and wives think that religion or spiritual values are abstract concepts in one's mind, but like many other matters in marriage, the spiritual dimension is often shown by specific behaviors. Until a husband and wife know what spirituality means to each other, it will be difficult for them to fulfill each other's spiritual needs.

Following is a communication exercise to help you discuss the spiritual aspects of your marriage.

Communication about Spiritual Issues

Instructions: Look over the following list and decide together which sentences you will discuss. Then take turns completing the sentences. After you have discussed one sentence, select another one and do the same:

1. I feel the closest to you spiritually when _____.
2. I feel closest to the Lord when _____.
3. I feel the most inspired when _____.
4. Religion helps me enjoy life because _____.
5. The religious beliefs that mean the most to me are _____.
6. Participation in Church activities is important to me because _____.
7. The things I'd like to do more (with you) in the spiritual area are _____.
8. The ways you could help me attain my spiritual needs are _____.
9. The most spiritual experiences I have had thus far in my life are _____.
10. The most spiritual experiences we have had together thus far in our marriage are _____.
11. The way I feel about prayer is _____.
12. Our prayers have been answered when _____.
13. We could increase our spiritual life together by _____.
14. Participation with other adults in religious activities is important because _____.
15. The times I feel most hopeful are _____.
16. The things that are the most worth living for right now are _____.
17. The most inspirational religious books I have read are _____.
18. We could develop spirituality in our children by _____.
19. What I really feel about the Lord is _____.
20. Other matters relating to spirituality I'd like to discuss with you are _____.

Princes of the Gentiles

Two of the most controversial passages in the Bible relating to marriage are Genesis 3:16, where God said unto Eve, "Thy desire shall be to thy husband, and he shall rule over thee," and

85

Ephesians 5:22, where Paul admonished, "Wives, submit your-selves unto your own husbands." These two scriptures seem to put women in a subservient position to men. And there is little question that in some cultures men have higher status than women.

But Paul also said that "the husband is the head of the wife, even as Christ is the head of the church" (Ephesians 5:23), suggesting that the leadership Jesus gave his church is the kind of leadership a husband should give his wife. What kind of leader was Jesus?

On one occasion the mother of James and John came to Jesus desiring that her sons be given greater recognition than the other disciples. She wanted one to sit on his right and the other to sit on his left in his kingdom. Jesus replied that they may not understand the rigors of true discipleship. Jesus replied, "Ye know that the princes of the Gentiles exercise dominion . . . , and they that are great exercise authority . . . . But it shall not be so among you: but whosoever will be great among you, let him be your minister; And whosoever will be chief among you, let him be your servant." (See Matthew 20:20-27.)

Just as in Biblical times, there are still "princes of Gentiles" who have dominion over others and exercise authority. Unfortunately, many of these "princes" want to exercise that dominion and authority over the women they marry. Those professing discipleship to Christ must remember that he said, "It shall not be so among you." (Matthew 20:26.) Jesus' followers would become great not by dominion and authority, but by becoming servants and ministers to others. And this is the model. A Christian husband should be "head" of his wife by ministering to her and serving her needs.

The relationship of Jesus and his disciples is also illustrated in an incident just prior to his crucifixion. At the time of the Feast of the Passover, Jesus admonished his disciples to love one another and then said, "Henceforth I call you not servants; for the servant knoweth not what his lord doeth: but I have called you *friends*; for all things that I have heard of my Father I have made known unto you." (John 15:15; italics added.) This friendship between Jesus and his disciples is another example for husbands and wives. I know of few better ways for a husband and wife to live together than as friends.

As mentioned in chapter 2, companionate or friendship love is a vital part of a husband-wife relationship. Perhaps more of our time in marriage is spent as friends than in any other way. There are times for romance, but most of our marriage is spent being friends.

Young people may become romantically involved with a person they may not even like. And after marriage, a friendship usually develops between the husband and wife. But sometimes it does not. I frequently advise young people approaching marriage to become friends before marriage. That way they won't have to run the risk of a friendship not emerging after marriage. There are too many married couples today who are not friends. They would rather spend time with almost anyone than each other. Couples must simply learn to be friends. I share the sentiments of Eda LeShan, who wrote: "One of the most valuable attributes of marriage is that one's partner can truly be one's best friend, and friendship was never more important. If one defines a friend as someone who loves you in spite of knowing your faults and weaknesses, and has even better dreams for your fulfillment than you have for yourself, it can surely be the foundation for what each of us needs most: . . . permission to quest for one's own identity."[2]

If anyone questions which is greater in the sight of God, husbands or wives, he or she ought to consider the words of Paul: "For as many of you as have been baptized into Christ have put on Christ. There is neither Jew nor Greek, there is neither bond nor free, *there is neither male nor female*: for ye are all one in Christ Jesus." (Galatians 3:27-28; italics added.) Paul also said, "Neither is the man without the woman, neither the woman without the man, in the Lord." (1 Corinthians 11:11.)

A Christian Concept of Love

Jesus said the ability to love others is the sign of true discipleship. (John 13:35.) This is particularly true for husbands

87

and wives. (See Colossians 3:19; Titus 2:4-5.) And John might have been speaking to husbands and wives when he wrote, "Beloved, let us love one another: for love is of God; and every one that loveth is born of God, and knoweth God. He that loveth not knoweth not God; for God is love. In this was manifested the love of God toward us, because that God sent his only begotten Son into the world, that we might live through him. Herein is love, not that we loved God, but that he loved us, and sent his Son to be the propitiation for our sins. Beloved, if God so loved us, we ought also to love one another." (1 John 4:7-11.)

I appreciate Paul's definition of love. He gives a fairly concise description of what love is and is not in 1 Corinthians 13:4-7:

Love

Is		*Is Not*
Patient	(Suffereth long)	Anxious
Kind	(Is kind)	Cruel
Supportive	(Envieth not)	Jealous
Modest	(Vaunteth not)	Boastful
Humble	(Not puffed up)	Arrogant
Polite	(Doth not behave unseemly)	Rude
Unselfish	(Seeketh not her own)	Demanding
Non-Defensive	(Not easily provoked)	Irritable
Trusting	(Thinketh no evil)	Suspicious
	(Rejoiceth not in iniquity	
Honest	but in truth)	Deceitful
Submissive	(Beareth all things)	Resistant
Confident	(Believeth all things)	Doubtful
Optimistic	(Hopeth all things)	Pessimistic
Permanent	(Endureth all things)	Conditional

When we become this kind of person, our charity or love "never faileth." (Verse 8.)

As I have studied these fourteen characteristics of love, I have become particularly impressed with the last four, bearing, believing, hoping, and enduring, and how they relate to a Christian marriage. These four words might be summed up in one word: commitment.

During the past decade we have seen the increasing popularity of short-term marriage—not for a few years, but for only a few months or even weeks. Some celebrities marry for only a few short days. My concern increases when I talk to newly married couples who, after one or two months, are ready to call it quits. Not long ago a young woman phoned me late at night (she actually woke me up) and wanted to know if we could talk for a few minutes. She began to cry and told me how unhappy she was in her marriage. Nothing seemed to be going right, and it wasn't at all like she thought it was going to be. After a few minutes, I finally got a chance to say something and asked her how long she had been married. There was a muffled cry, and then she responded, "Two weeks." Such cases are not uncommon.

I recently had the opportunity, along with an estimated one billion other people, to watch on television the wedding of Prince Charles and Lady Diana of Great Britain. Besides the pageantry of the ceremony, I was particularly impressed when the prince promised to marry Lady Diana "for better or worse, for richer or poorer, in sickness and in health." This, to me, is what bearing, believing, hoping, and enduring mean in marriage.

Bearing means that we will withstand the difficult times of marriage; we will not give up when things get a little bit rough, particularly during the first years of marriage.

Believing means that we have the confidence in ourselves, in each other, and in God to survive the difficult moments in married life.

Hoping means looking beyond the present. If we are "poor and sick" and things seem "worse" than ever before, we must be able to foresee better times ahead. If we are deeply in debt, we have to envision the time when we will be out of debt. Hope has been defined as the ability to tie a knot and hang on when you come to the end of your rope.

Enduring means that love is permanent. We are going to endure some hardships together. Our love will not depend on changing moods and situations. We will endure all we can, if possible "all things," as Paul says. Of course, in some situations endurance may be impossible.

89

Latter-day Saints have a special understanding of what marriage should be like as they take upon themselves the covenants of eternal marriage in the temple. As Elder David O. McKay said, "The love of husband and wife is an eternal bond, not sealed lightly in frivolity or passion but entered into by premeditation, careful observation, sacred association and prayer. (*Conference Report*, April 1930, p. 82.)

I was once speaking with a group of Latter-day Saint couples about commitment, belief, and hope in marriage. One woman said she and her husband had been married for seven years. They had experienced a particularly difficult marriage because of sickness, irregular work, and several other problems. She said there was one quotation that had saved their marriage. They had read it often during the difficult years, and she read it for us: "Search diligently, pray always, and be believing, and all things shall work together for your good, if ye walk uprightly and remember the covenant wherewith ye have covenanted one with another." (Doctrine and Covenants 90:24.) That is real commitment!

Confess Your Faults

Recently, a young man who had been married only a few months was describing to me the adjustments he and his wife had made. He concluded, "You might say we have a strange and wonderful relationship—she's strange and I'm wonderful."

The tendency to blame one's spouse for problems and to see one's self as flawless is all too common. Why are we so willing to criticize our spouse's inadequacies and to deny our own faults?

To overcome this tendency, the apostle James encouraged the early Christians to "confess your faults one to another, and pray one for another, that ye may be healed." (James 5:16.) This may be good advice for husbands and wives.

It is not uncommon in marriage counseling for a husband and wife to come in with a long list of complaints of what the other person is doing to cause stress in their relationship. Both partners can name the times, places, and dates when their spouse did something to offend them. Yet, when asked about their own faults, they deny any wrongdoing. Of course, if nothing else, they have contributed to the stress by allowing it to evolve to the point where it now is.

The inability to recognize one's own faults apparently was a common tendency during the time of Jesus. Drawing on his familiarity with carpentry, he commented on this tendency, using the analogy of a speck of sawdust, a mote, and a large piece of wood, a beam:

> Judge not, that ye be not judged. For with what judgment ye judge, ye shall be judged: and with what measure ye mete, it shall be measured to you again. And why beholdest thou the mote that is in thy brother's eye, but considerest not the beam that is in thine own eye? Or how wilt thou say to thy brother, Let me pull out the mote out of thine eye; and, behold, a beam is in thine own eye? Thou hypocrite, first cast out the beam out of thine own eye; and then shalt thou see clearly to cast out the mote out of thy brother's eye. (Matthew 7:1-5.)

By learning to acknowledge our own faults, we are much more likely to help our spouses change than by constantly keeping their inadequacies before them. The likelihood of a person admitting his own weaknesses is usually much greater when his spouse is willing to acknowledge weaknesses as well. By admitting errors and showing willingness to work for reconciliation, you have acknowledged to your spouse what both of you probably recognize: you are two strange people with a potentially wonderful relationship.

James not only encouraged us to confess our faults to each other but encouraged us to pray for each other's weaknesses. It is much easier to pray for the inadequacies of another, as did the Pharisee with the publican (see Luke 18:9-14), than it is to kneel down together as husband and wife and request your spouse to pray in behalf of one of your faults. Jesus said, "Every one that exalteth himself shall be abased; and he that humbleth himself shall be exalted." (Luke 18:14.)

Offenses Will Come

Frequently I encounter both married and single people who believe it is possible for a husband and wife to live together year after year without raising their voices or having any kind of confrontation. There are such marriages that may mature over time, or else the husband and wife may be so distant emotionally that they don't care to become involved in any way whatsoever with each other. But for most husbands and wives, there will be times when they will both offend and be offended. Jesus knew this. He said, "It is impossible but that offences will come." (Luke 17:1.) He also said that people should forgive each other even if offended seven times daily! (See Luke 17:1-10.) Few of us get to that point, but some may come close.

Because Jesus knew that offenses would be given and received by his disciples, he taught reconciliation and forgiveness, both of which are important in marriage.

Reconciliation. With slight adaptation, Jesus' teachings on reconciliation can be applied to husband and wife. For instance, in the following scripture, substitute the word *spouse* for *brother.* Jesus said, "Moreover if thy brother shall trespass against thee, go and tell him his fault between thee and him alone: if he shall hear thee, thou hast gained thy brother." (Matthew 18:15.)

Here Jesus says that if one is offended, he has the obligation to go to the person giving the offense and seek reconciliation. When I discuss this concept with couples, they usually say that this teaching seems inappropriate. Why should the offended person seek out the offender? People often think, "They are the ones who hurt my feelings! They should come to me!"

However, most of us can remember a time when we offended someone unintentionally, and we appreciated the person coming to us to make us aware of the offense.

I remember that once as a Church administrator I publicly praised a person who had just been released from a Church assignment. I meant well in so doing and thought nothing of it the rest of the day. That evening I received a phone call from another member of the Church who, in a gentle way, let me know that I had offended him. He said that a few weeks earlier he too had been released from a similar Church assignment and that I had failed to mention his release or recognize his service. I appreciated the phone call because I had unknowingly offended him, and his call gave me the chance to repent and make amends.,

Another reason to seek out others when they offend us is that as we sit and stew and smolder, the offense grows in our minds. People frequently ask me when to seek out an offending party and when to just "forgive and forget." I usually answer that if the offense is causing one to lose sleep or disrupting one's daily activities, he should seek reconciliation with the other person.

We should let our spouses know, in a kind way, when they have offended us. Otherwise, they may continue to offend unknowingly.

Not only should we seek out an offending person for reconciliation; Jesus also taught that when we are the offender, we should go to the person we have offended. In the Sermon on the Mount, he said, "Therefore if thou bring thy gift to the altar, and there rememberest that thy brother hath ought against thee; leave there thy gift before the altar, and go thy way; first be reconciled to thy brother, and then come and offer thy gift." (Matthew 5:23-24.)

In other words, we should reconcile our differences with others, and then we will be ready to worship the Lord. Suppose that you are driving to church, but you and your spouse are not talking to each other because you said something about her always being late. Since you offended her, you have the obligation to seek reconciliation. But as the offended party, she also is obliged to work things out with you. Jesus implied that it is difficult to worship when we have ill feelings toward others. This is particularly true with our husbands or wives.

Jesus also mentioned the importance of seeking reconciliation promptly: "Agree with thine adversary quickly, whiles thou art in the way with him; lest at any time the adversary deliver thee to the judge, and the judge deliver thee to the officer, and thou be cast into prison. Verily I say unto thee, Thou shalt

93

by no means come out thence, till thou hast paid the uttermost farthing." (Matthew 5:25-26.)

Whether we are the offended or the offender, we have the obligation to seek out the other party for reconciliation. We should do so while we have the opportunity. If we do not, we put ourselves into an emotional prison. Conflict usually gets worse if not confronted and resolved.

The Apostle Paul gave similar advice: "Let not the sun go down upon your wrath." (Ephesians 4:26.) This is where the adage "Never go to bed angry" comes from. When my wife and I were first married, we tried to work out our differences late at night before going to bed. But we never could. We found that by getting some sleep and then discussing our differences the next morning when we were alert, we could quickly resolve our concerns. Most of the time, our differences the night before were so petty that upon waking we couldn't even remember what they were.

"Let not the sun go down upon your wrath" means that we should resolve our differences promptly, perhaps within twenty-four or forty-eight hours. By dealing with our "adversary" quickly, we can avoid the emotional prison that Jesus decribed.

Forgiveness. Someone once said, "If you were bitten by a snake, you can either chase the snake or get rid of the poison." Most of us, when offended, want to retaliate, or chase the snake. Perhaps there is wisdom in leaving the snake to itself and concentrating on getting rid of the venom. This is what forgiveness is all about.

When Jesus gave the Sermon on the Mount, he taught a higher law than that lived by his disciples. The Mosaic law prescribed "eye for eye, tooth for tooth." (Exodus 21:24.) Jesus taught, however, that we should not retaliate, but turn the other cheek. (Matthew 5:39.)

As a young man, I had a difficult time understanding this teaching. But I failed to learn early in life that the best way to end a confrontation is to not retaliate. What I did learn in my rural upbringing was that if one lives by the sword, he dies by the sword.

Not retaliating admittedly takes self-control, but for husbands and wives, it is a must. Two people seeking vengeance on each other will soon destroy each other, physically, emotionally, or both. And we learn not to retaliate by forgiving. It is true that if retaliation does not occur, the offending party may benefit. But the principle of forgiveness was meant for the offended more than for the offender.

After explaining the principle of forgiveness in my marriage class not long ago, I challenged the students to seek out someone they resented and to initiate reconciliation by going as the offended party to the offender. I suggested that they tell the person that they frankly forgave them, if possible, and then see what happened.

One student, divorced for several years, later reported that she had had many resentful feelings toward her former husband. Since she and her young son had not seen him for a long time, the resentment had grown and was becoming unmanageable. She wrote to her former husband and let him know that his absence since the divorce had caused her much suffering. She told him she forgave him for what he had done, or failed to do.

Then something interesting happened. She realized that she too was part of the problem. So she confessed her faults and asked her former husband to forgive her. She signed the letter and sent it to his last known address.

She was not certain her former husband would receive the letter. But the moment she dropped the letter in the mailbox, it was as if an enormous load had been taken off her mind. She had experienced what it means to get rid of the venom rather than chasing the snake.

As a marriage counselor, it is amazing to me how a husband and wife can offend each other and then carry that resentment for years. One woman described to me something her husband had done nearly eighteen years earlier. She had never been able to forgive him. If she had sought reconciliation when the offense was first committed, she might have worked through her resentment and frustrations. As it was, she had let it go and been resentful for nearly two decades of marriage. It was obvious that the venom had poisoned their relationship.

There are three sentences that work miracles in marriage: "I love you," "I'm sorry," "Please forgive me." While these are difficult to say, they indicate a willingness to acknowledge faults and a desire to be reconciled. Husbands and wives should frequently use these sentences.

Jesus prayed, "Forgive us our debts, as we forgive our debtors." (Matthew 6:12.) And at the end of his prayer, he reminded his disciples, "If ye forgive men their trespasses, your heavenly Father will also forgive you: but if ye forgive not men their trespasses, neither will your Father forgive your trespasses." (Matthew 6:14-15.)

Failure of a husband and wife to forgive each other may cause them not to be forgiven for their own sins. Literally, "with what measure ye mete, it shall be measured to you again." (Matthew 7:2.)

Defraud Not

After counseling many couples who either contemplate divorce or actually divorce, I have noticed a pattern that precedes most separations. There are frequent arguments, sporadic separations, talk or threats of divorce, and prolonged periods of time, usually months, with little or no sexual interaction. While there is much more to marriage than intimacy, it is usually an excellent barometer of the well-being of a marriage.

Paul warned against withholding sexual fulfillment in marriage. His counsel, given nearly two thousand years ago, is still valid. In my years of counseling, I have seldom found a marriage that was both stable and satisfying unless both husband and wife were receiving some degree of sexual satisfaction.

Writing to the early saints in Corinth, Paul warned against fornication and then admonished, "Let the husband render unto the wife due benevolence: and likewise also the wife unto the husband. The wife hath not power of her own body, but the husband: and likewise also the husband hath not power of his own body, but the wife. Defraud ye not one the other, except it be with consent for a time, that ye may give yourselves to fasting and prayer; and come together again, that Satan tempt you not for your incontinency." (1 Corinthians 7:3-5.)

Paul encouraged couples to give to each other their sexual or conjugal rights. That he spoke to both husbands and wives shows that women and men have equal rights to sexual fulfillment. He suggested that the body is not for individual gratification, but for the fulfillment of one's husband or wife. He also wisely encouraged husbands and wives not to withhold sexual fulfillment unless both partners agree to abstain for a short time for fasting and prayer. But he warned them not to abstain too long lest they should be tempted in their sexual desires.

Some people may "defraud" their husband or wife because they have a difficult time reconciling their sexual feelings with their religious beliefs. They may not realize that God created the human body (Genesis 1:26-27), including the basic sexual drive of men and women. After the human body with all its marvelous functions had been created, "God saw every thing that he had made, and behold, it was very good." (Genesis 1:31.) He then commanded his creations to "multiply, and replenish the earth." (Genesis 1:28.)

Furthermore, in order to overcome loneliness (Genesis 2:18), Adam and Eve became "one flesh." (Genesis 2:24.) Becoming "one" involves many dimensions of marriage, including the sexual act. And sexual unity is still as essential in marriage as it was thousands of years ago.

It is interesting to me that the word *sex* is not found in the Bible. Yet physical intimacy is described in the scriptures. The word *know*, meaning "to become acquainted with," is often used in the scriptures to describe the oneness that can develop through sexual interaction. This word is first used in Genesis 4:1: "And Adam knew Eve his wife; and she conceived, and bare Cain."

Finally, the Bible admonishes husbands and wives to seek their sexual fulfillment with each other, and in so doing, to take pleasure and rejoice. Sarah, wife of Abraham, referred to the conjugal relationship when she asked the Lord, "Shall I have pleasure?" (Genesis 18:12.) And Solomon admonished, "Rejoice with the wife of thy youth." (Proverbs 5:18.)

6

SENSITIVITY

Oscar Wilde once said, "Each man kills the thing he loves," and the irony of that statement provokes much thought. Perhaps we often take the greatest liberties with those relationships that are most important to us.

We can kill something in one of two ways: (1) by an abrupt act of violence (abuse) or (2) through failure to provide the elements essential for growth (neglect). Both methods are efficient, with the first being sudden and easily noticeable. The second, however, is more subtle, prolonged, and difficult to detect. It was obvious from the numerous letters I received from wives that they wanted and expected greater sensitivity, concern, appreciation, or awareness from their husbands. In other words, they didn't want their relationships to die because of neglect.

We are perhaps more vulnerable in marriage than in any other relationship. A husband and wife are psychologically and emotionally naked before each other. They have no pretenses and no facades because facades erode quickly. One's true self soon emerges after the wedding ceremony and a spouse's weaknesses and strengths emerge. Marriage usually brings out the best and the worst in people.

No one knows a person better than his spouse, and this knowledge can be a two-edged sword. It can be used to help a spouse become a better person by capitalizing on strengths and overcoming weaknesses. Or, as is sadly and frequently the case, it can be used to cut down a spouse by pointing out weaknesses and ignoring strengths.

Here are some comments wives made about their husbands' sensitivity, or lack of it, as the men leave and return home each day:

"One of the things I would really appreciate in the future is the total undivided attention of my husband when we meet after our day's activities. I would like to sit down with him right then and really try to understand each other's experiences and feelings. Perhaps that sort of listening or sensitivity is what we lack most in our marriage. But when he listens—not just to what I am saying, but to how I am feeling—then I know he really loves me."

"I wish my husband would ask me, "How was your day?" or as he leaves in the morning, say, 'I hope you have a good day with the children.' Usually it is the other way around, with me saying something to him."

"It would be nice if my husband would come home from work, look into my eyes, and ask me how I feel, how was my busy day, and then give me a kiss and a long hug."

And wives need encouragement. They reported:

"I want my husband to tell me more often that I look nice or that he likes my hair, outfit, etc."

"Once in a while my husband tells me I look nice and compliments me on a meal. Usually he supports me in the things that I want to do concerning my own life."

"Husbands need to understand that a wife and mother's day is very busy and that we need an encouraging word. Don't judge us critically, but try to understand and talk to us about various matters."

"My husband praises me in public and among his friends. He seldom demeans, jokes, or criticizes me around others or reveals our personal problems or inadequacies to others."

"Usually he praises and gives appreciation for me privately and publicly. He is always telling our children what a great mother they have and what a terrific cook she is."

When wives are not feeling well, they would like extra concern, sensitivity, and help, as indicated in these comments:

"My husband is quick to sense when I'm not feeling well and even offers to come home from his work to help out. Although I've never had him do this, it makes me feel that I'm his first priority and come first in his life."

"There are a few times I remember that I was really sick, almost unable to get out of bed, let alone take care of the children, get meals, or anything else. My husband was able to take right over and handle everything and even has taken off work to stay home and help me. I always felt very grateful to him and very much appreciated his willingness and ability to help."

"My husband cooks breakfast every Saturday morning while I relax and get some extra sleep. Also, there are times he will step in and help when I'm not feeling well. A sick mom goes to bed at our house."

Wives want a husband who will help with the difficult household work. Women need more help and special attention when they are working, sick, or pregnant:

"I wish my husband would show more kindness and caring the next time we have a baby. After taking me home from the hospital he should stick around and help. Sometimes he gets angry at me for not getting the dishes done promptly after breakfast and the house cleaned up after I get home from the hospital. He needs to be more understanding of the fact I just can't bounce and bustle around the house immediately after having a baby."

And sometimes there are just bad days for wives. According to one wife, husbands need to be more sensitive during these times as well:

"In the future I hope my husband will be more understanding when he comes home and finds the house in a disaster. I try hard, but some days just come when a child is ill and hangs on me all day and cries. The phone rings constantly and unexpected company keeps coming. My entire day goes down the tube, the house is a wreck, and my nerves are shot! It hurts me and shows a lack of concern when my husband comes home and says, 'Can't you organize things better and keep this house clean? What a mess!' Far better would be a smile and words like, 'My, but you've had a rough day today! Can I help?' I resent his thinking that I'd slept all day."

These comments suggest that husbands need to be more sensitive to wives on many occasions. Following are discussions of some of those times.

Leaving home. After graduating from college, I began my teaching career at Davis High School in Kaysville. There I met Ken Sheffield, who was just completing a long and successful career as a teacher and administrator.

One thing my wife Susan and I noticed about Ken and his wife Lucile was the concern and attentiveness they showed each other. They confided that they were particularly sensitive about their last words spoken as they parted each morning.

What they said and how they said it often set the tone for the whole day. They took care not to leave each other in the morning with negative thoughts or feelings.

As a newly married couple, Susan and I thought this was a good idea and have tried to incorporate it into our own marriage. And most of the time, we have been successful.

A poem that reminds me of Ken and Lucile is "Our Own," by Margaret E. Sangster:

If I had known in the morning
How wearily all the day
The words unkind would trouble my mind
That I said when you went away,
I had been more careful, darling,
Nor given you needless pain;
But we vex our own with look and tone
We may never take back again.

For though in the quiet evening
You may give me the kiss of peace,
Yet it well might be that never for me
The pain of the heart should cease!
How many go forth at morning
Who never come home at night!
And hearts have broken for harsh words spoken
That sorrow can ne'er set right.

We have careful thoughts for the stranger,
And smiles for the sometime guest;
But oft for "our own" the bitter tone,
Though we love our own the best.
Ah! lips with the curve impatient,
Ah! brow with the shade of scorn,
'Twere a cruel fate, were the night too late
To undo the work of the morn![1]

Arriving home. One of the most intriguing aspects of marriage is that two people can experience the same event and yet have entirely different perceptions of what happened. When I come home from work, I think of myself as a knight on a white horse who has been out slaying dragons all day. The only thing that could add to the analogy would be if a moat were dug around our house, a drawbridge were lowered, and the children all lined up and did a trumpet fanfare as I arrived.

Susan, however, sees things differently. She perceives my arrival as being more like the U.S. Cavalry charging in with a bugle call to rescue her from the frequent ambushes of our children. In other words, help has finally arrived.

While this illustration may sound somewhat facetious, it demonstrates something we realized early in our marriage. We found we were often insensitive to what each other had experienced during the day.

Some time ago I was away from home three or four days and missed my family a great deal. I was anxious to get home, but upon returning was disappointed at my welcome. None of the children came to greet me as they were preoccupied with some other activity. My absence had not been noticed as much by my family, it seemed, as it had by me. Susan was unusually quiet during the next few hours, which added to my dismay.

Later that evening I told Susan how disappointed I was. She then told me what had happened while I had been gone. The car wouldn't start, the washing machine had broken down, the hot water heater worked only part of the time, and the children had been less than cooperative. These things had made our time apart difficult for her.

Both husbands and wives confront difficult situations. Perhaps marriage would be less hectic if we were more sensitive to each other's problems when we meet in the evening.

Appreciation

One wife wrote to me:

"I think what women really want is appreciation. Whether we want to admit it or not, our lives are spent in service to our husbands, children, neighbors, church, school, and community. We don't get a paycheck, raise, or promotion for rendering these services.

103

And then we sometimes are asked to do more. Once in a while we get praised for these things, but sometimes it becomes hollow and meaningless. On occasion, we get a genuine thanks and honest appreciation. I can keep going a long time for a few well-timed *thank yous*. If my husband wants to give me something to satisfy my inner-most desires, he could say thank you more often. This could come in the form of notes, or hugs, or kisses, or a special intimate evening. It can be a wink or a few words said. It can be stopping during the middle of his day to call me for no other reason than "just because." It could be a dozen other things that, surprisingly enough, don't cost large sums of money—just a little time and effort. Just knowing I am still a part of his thoughts and feelings, that I am an integral part of his life, would be great. It would keep my 'gas tank' full."

As husbands, do we express enough gratitude to our wives? Psychologist William James once wrote a book on human needs. Some years later, after the book was published, he commented that he had forgotten to include the greatest need of all—the need for appreciation. Perhaps that is why he later wrote, "The deepest principle of human nature is the craving to be appreciated."

Since that time others have also suggested that appreciation is one of the most positive gestures one person can make to another. But if this is so, why is sincere appreciation so infrequently expressed in some marriages and altogether missing in others? Is it because we do not appreciate each other, or is it because we do not make the effort to express our appreciation?

In their book *Relationships in Marriage and Family*,[2] Dr. Nick Stinnet and Dr. James Walters note, "The records of marriage and family counseling clinics suggest that many marital complaints and problems stem from a lack of feeling appreciated. A severe lack of appreciation for a marriage partner can place the marriage relationship in danger of being terminated. For example, when a wife feels that her husband does not appreciate her, her ego is threatened. Her sense of worth is attacked. Lack of appreciation or ridicule can easily result in a wife feeling resentment, bitterness, and even hatred toward her husband." (P. 85.)

Sincere appreciation says, "You are a person of worth and dignity. You have much to contribute to others." It also says, "I am interested enough in you to see and acknowledge your positive qualities." Expressions of appreciation strengthen relationships, and their importance cannot be overemphasized. Nearly everyone has good qualities that can be appreciated by others.

President Spencer W. Kimball said:

> Love is like a flower, and, like the body, it needs constant feeding. The mortal body would soon be emaciated and die if there were not frequent feedings. The tender flower would wither and die without food and water. And so love, also, cannot be expected to last forever unless it is continually fed with portions of love, the manifestation of esteem and admiration, the expressions of gratitude, and the consideration of unselfishness. . . .
>
> Many couples permit their marriages to become stale and their love to grow cold like old bread or worn-out jokes or cold gravy. Certainly the foods most vital for love are consideration, kindness, thoughtfulness, concern, expressions of affection, embraces of appreciation, admiration, pride, companionship, confidence, faith, partnership, equality, and dependence.[3]

Elder Neal A. Maxwell said, "If another person only had in his storehouse of deserved self-esteem what you had put there, what would he have to draw upon and to sustain him?"[4]

If you are a husband, put down this book and go find your wife. Put your arms around her and tell her how much you appreciate her. Give her some specific reasons why. You might even show your appreciation by helping her in some way. But you should have some household ammonia nearby to revive her in case she faints.

Wives and Self-Esteem

One of the critical issues in marriage today is self-esteem. Most marriage counselors would agree on at least two things: We each are basically responsible for our own self-esteem, and our self-esteem is greatly influenced by how we think others perceive us.

Perhaps no one knows us better than our spouses, and the insights they have about us can be used to build our self-esteem or to destroy it.

In his book *What Wives Wish Their Husbands Knew about Women,*[5] Dr. James Dobson, family specialist at the University of Southern California School of Medicine, has reported that low self-esteem is a major problem facing women in America today. He has asked more than ten thousand women to respond to a simple questionnaire; fifty percent reported low self-esteem to be their worst problem. Over eighty percent of the women listed low self-esteem among their top five problems. Dr. Dobson notes, "This finding is perfectly consistent with my own observations and expectations; even in seemingly healthy and happily married young women, personal inferiority and self-doubt cut the deepest and leave the most wicked scars. Feelings of inadequacy, lack of confidence, and a certainty of worthlessness have become a way of life, or too often, a way of despair for millions of American women." (P. 22.)

Marriage counselors have become acutely aware that a husband or wife can often contribute to or be the major cause of a spouse's low self-esteem. If married people want to belittle each other they know the pet words, the old jokes, and the hackneyed phrases that can rattle their spouses on cue. They know what to say and when to hurt each other's feelings and lower self-esteem.

But on the positive side, couples can learn to build each other's self-esteem if they desire. If Dr. Dobson's findings are correct, this is particularly important for husbands to learn to do. But how do they do it?

Dr. Carlfred Broderick, marriage counselor, also from the University of Southern California, notes in his recent book *Marriage and the Family,*[6] "Both research and experience show

106

us there are many things one can do directly to help increase a partner's sense of worth. Some techniques are so well known that it is almost embarrassing to recount them here: a compliment, a non-demanding touch, an appreciative look, a smile. Perhaps one might add remembering important things, avoiding hurtful or sensitive areas, and paying attention when the other person is talking. Yet despite the almost universal awareness of the power and value of these gestures, they are missing altogether from many relationships and exceeding rare in many more." (Pp. 80-81.)

Broderick believes that many young people never saw these things in their parents' home. Others, he states, may withhold these gestures to manipulate their spouses. They may also refrain from building the esteem of their spouses in order to feel superior to them. Or they may build up their partner's esteem only later to reveal that they never meant any of the good things they said, thereby contributing to their own and their spouses' cynicism.

A husband should learn how to increase his wife's self-esteem by giving her a storehouse of praise from which she can draw as needed. In addition, he needs to be particularly sensitive when her esteem is low. We all have days when we do not feel our best.

Because of hormonal changes, women have feelings that men sometimes do not understand. These changes occur monthly during the menstrual cycle, with pregnancy, and during menopause. All can cause moodiness. During these times a husband should be particularly sensitive to the needs and feelings of his wife.

Dr. Dobson reports, "Self-esteem in women is directly related to estrogen levels; hence, it fluctuates predictably through the 28-day cycle." Estrogen levels in women are at their lowest point, as is self-esteem, immediately before, during, and after menstruation. The level of estrogen peaks near the time of ovulation, at mid-cycle. This is also the time most women experience the greatest emotional optimism and self-confidence." (P. 151.)

Similar symptoms may occur during pregnancy and after

childbirth, when some women experience post-partum depression, and during menstruation.

Among the emotional symptoms often accompanying menopause are prolonged depression, low self-esteem, low frustration tolerance, and inappropriate emotional responses such as crying for no reason or depression during relatively good times. Others are irregular sleep patterns, inability to concentrate, and difficulty in remembering.

Tremendous Trifles

We need to be sensitive in seemingly small matters in marriage. Someone once called them marital termites. In almost every prolonged relationship, including marriage, there are usually things people do that irritate each other. And just because they appear to be insignificant to others does not mean they should or will be insignificant to you.

I had a roommate in college who used to flip his ear while we were studying, and it was highly irritating. Once I had a secretary who had been married just three weeks. I asked her how everything was going. She said the relationship was going well, but then she paused. "There is one thing he does that I can't stand. He always leaves the toilet lid up. And if there is anything I can't stand, it's walking into a bathroom and looking down into a toilet."

If couples are honest with each other, they will admit that minor incidents lead to major annoyances. In his book *Marriage*,[7] Dr. Robert O. Blood, Jr., notes that a tremendous trifle is anything that irritates one party but is a mere trifle to the other. To outsiders also these often seem trifling—the cap left off the toothpaste, dirty socks on the bedroom floor, or slurped soup. They seem especially trifling to offenders if they are unaware of their behavior.

Dr. Blood suggests we should not underestimate the impact of tremendous trifles: "Tremendous trifles cause tremendous damage. When anxiety in the threatened partner explodes in denunciation of the offending spouse, he reciprocates defensively. Conflict and mutual recrimination become chronic if the trouble is literally an everyday affair. The fact that the issue is trifling makes it harder to deal with rationally. Major tragedies call out the best in people, but petty irritants are handled in petty ways." (P. 355.)

There are at least four things you can do about tremendous trifles. First, explain to your spouse the annoying behavior and ask him or her to change the habits. Second, if possible, segregate the trouble. Buy two toothpaste tubes and label them "His" and "Hers." Place clothes hampers in strategic places to catch dirty socks or underwear. Get to the bathroom first in the morning so you won't have to face the whiskers in the sink. Third, try humor if both of you can laugh about the incident. Fourth, if your spouse simply will not or cannot change, you may have to increase your tolerance and simply learn to be forgiving. After all, if you ask, you will find that your spouse has a list of your tremendous trifles.

A Weighty Matter

There are, perhaps, few other areas in which husbands and wives need to have greater sensitivity than in weight gain. This is particularly true for women during and after pregnancy. But physical and emotional problems from excessive weight gain also occur at other times. And a marriage partner can be either a help or hindrance during these times.

Most husbands and wives go through a periodic "Dump the Plump" campaign, when one or both try to lose weight. For some this seems to be a continuous process, while for others it is on-again, off-again. There are hundreds of programs and gimmicks for dieters as evidenced by a quick glance at the advertising sections of newspapers and magazines or the yellow pages of the phone book. Have you ever stopped to think, however, that a husband's or wife's weight may be related to their marital relationship?

Sometimes wives gain weight and their husbands tell them to take it off or else. Not knowing what the "or else" entails, they go on a fanatic campaign to lose weight and save their marriage. Little do most husbands realize that there is an inverse correlation between how frequently they ask their wives how much they weigh and the actual weight loss. The more frequently husbands ask, the less weight wives lose.

There are psychological reasons for being overweight. In a few instances, a wife may be afraid of intimacy or has become nonchalant about the relationship. Because of many men's preoccupation with how women look, several extra pounds on a woman may make her less sexually desirable, by design, to her husband. Some women were sexually abused as children and are so terrified of intimacy as adults that they work hard to stay overweight so that they become less attractive.

In her recent book *People Around You Can Make You Fat*,[8] Dr. Lee Headley, Los Angeles therapist, notes:

> I have observed it to be rather typical in marriage situations to find an overweight woman married to a man who was seemingly calm, competent, and secure. Looking at such a marriage from the outside, it seemed that the overweight woman was lucky to have a husband like that, and it appeared that she was quite dependent on him.
>
> Looking at the marriage from the inside, the husband was often not nearly as secure and self-operating as he seemed, and needed to have a woman who would always be there for him because she had no other option. He was often as uncertain of himself as she was of herself, perhaps more so. Although a couple may never talk about what really goes on, the overweight woman may realize that thinness would jeopardize her husband's security as well as her own, and since she feels responsible for him, she may hesitate to upset the whole apple cart by getting thin. (P. 208.)

Sometimes a spouse is a hindrance to a partner who is dieting. For example, a husband may try to help his wife by acting as a coach and making frequent suggestions as to how she could improve. This, however, frequently leads to resentment by the dieter.

A spouse may try to be a referee who blows the whistle at every infraction of a weight loss rule. He or she may act as a scorekeeper and keep a daily record of every pound lost or gained. But a partner best helps a spouse lose weight by being a cheerleader at the sidelines, applauding his or her efforts. Perhaps a partner could encourage his or her spouse rather than constantly remind him or her about a weight problem. Cheerleaders often do the most good when the game is not going too well.

Marital Sand Traps

Each afternoon as I drive home from the University, I pass a golf course. People seem to be enjoying themselves with their drives, chips, putts, and so forth. And then there are the sand traps.

Golfers in sand traps do unusual things. They become angry and expend unnecessary time, energy, and emotion trying to get themselves out. Perhaps they should use greater effort to avoid sand traps altogether.

Marriage partners also tend to get into their own special kinds of sand traps. Almost every couple seems to have sensitive areas where unnecessary time, energy, and emotions are expended in unproductive efforts. And, as in golf, most of these sand traps could be avoided with a little skill and foresight.

What are some of the sand traps in your marriage? On what do you and your spouse spend unnecessary rounds of repeated confrontation? What are some of the things you say or do that cause tension?

In their book Me and You and Us,[9] Dr. Gerald Smith and Alice Phillips list some common areas of sensitivity in marriage: becoming preoccupied with work, forgetting to buy groceries, making the same point over and over, reading the paper while listening or half-listening, accepting a dinner invitation without first checking with a partner, agreeing to visit some people and then complaining about doing it, being too rational or uninvolved during conversation, nagging, the husband comparing his wife to his mother, going to a party and not

111

spending much time with the spouse, and a partner saying "I agree" when he doesn't agree and just wants to keep the peace.

We should approach the sensitive areas in marriage like someone else's feet in a dark movie theater. Avoid unnecessary contact, relax, and enjoy what we were originally seeking.

7

AUTONOMY

In *The Prophet*, Kahlil Gibran wrote:
Give your hearts, but not into each other's keeping
For only the hand of Life can contain your hearts.
And stand together yet not too near together;
For the pillars of the temple stand apart,
And the oak tree and the cypress grow not in each other's
    shadow.[1]
The thoughts expressed in these few lines raise a very interesting question about marriage. How much time should husbands and wives spend together? Wives want and need time with their husbands. But must all the hours a husband and wife are away from work, children, and other responsibilities be spent together?

Wives Expect Autonomy

It was indicated in many of the letters from wives that they appreciated being involved in activities that did not always directly relate to husband, children, or family. In addition, in the "Profile of a Loving Husband," autonomy ranked seventh out of twenty items.

One of the best ways a husband can help his wife have more autonomy is to help her with her many responsibilities.

Here are some comments from wives about autonomy:

"I would appreciate having a little more help with the children. It would be nice occasionally to have my husband just take them for a drive—anything—to give me some time for myself. There is also the problem of bedtime. He could say, 'I'll get the kids into bed tonight so you can go read or watch television.' "

"I think women like to be treated as distinct individuals who are unique, intelligent, and important. We like someone to talk to us and listen to us. We need rewards and recognition just as our husbands do. We like to be included in the planning and decisions that affect our lives."

And apparently numerous other husbands do help their wives find the time they need to do things alone:

"I appreciate my husband's constant encouragement to find some activity that would take me out of the home for a time each week while he cares for the children. This results in my being able to take several classes at the University. While I view the physical and financial support as a great manifestation of love, surpassing that has been the emotional support and pride of a husband who delights in my accomplishments."

"My husband encouraged me to take voice lessons, something I have wanted to do for years. All I needed was a little encouragement to do so."

"My husband respects my intelligence and considers my point of view and trusts me to make major decisions while he is gone."

"My husband builds up my self-confidence and sense of personal worth. Whenever I decide I want to improve something about myself, he supports me with the encouragement, cooperation, financial resources, and time to do what I desire to do. Sometimes he will work right along with me."

An American Peculiarity

In his book *The Individual, Marriage and the Family*,[2] Lloyd Saxton notes that in America expectations about husband-wife togetherness are different than in any other country: "The expectation is to marry to "live happily ever after" in mutual companionship and emotional support. This cultural ideal of togetherness, which is especially prevalent in the middle class, is a romantic illusion in that it emphasizes unrealistic goals: the exclusive possession of the love object and almost complete identification with it." (P. 251.)

Once couples realize that even between the closest human beings infinite distances exist, they can learn to appreciate their differences as well as their similarities. Robert O. Blood notes, "Couples must share their basic values and key activities, but this does not prevent them from going their separate ways the rest of the time. . . . Happy are those who find it possible to maintain a flexible bond between growing personalities. For them, marriage is a liberating force and a creative achievement."[3]

Conflict may arise if either husband or wife expects the other to give up all previous interests, activities, and attitudes that he or she cannot share. Stable, fulfilling marriages will likely result if couples build their relationships on the expectation that all must grow as individuals, maintaining individual interests present at the beginning of the marriage in addition to developing new interests after marriage that may or may not be shared.

A Time and a Season

According to Ecclesiastes 3:1-8, there is a time for every purpose under heaven. And part of that is a "time to embrace, and a time to refrain from embracing [or, in the Hebrew, to be

115

far from each other]." There are times for husbands and wives to be together and times for them to be apart.

I have had some fascinating discussions about autonomy in my marriage classes. Students' expectations vary widely. Some feel that every free moment should be spent with their spouses while others want a great deal of time to pursue personal interests.

Until recently, husbands have expected and usually received the most autonomy in marriage. Their jobs have taken them away from home. For many, there are conventions and nights out with the boys or weekends hunting and fishing. Sports takes a lot of time for men. One wife suggested that her husband be declared legally dead if he watched three consecutive football games on television.

With all his time for self or friends, many husbands are insensitive to the desires of their wives. A husband may argue that when he has to be gone, his wife is able to stay at home. While this is true, she usually has to care for the home and children as well as some of the husband's responsibilities while he is gone. All this time at home can bring about "cabin fever," which can only be cured by getting away from the "cabin" for a few days. Going home to mother has usually been viewed with disdain by most husbands, but a few days visiting parents or friends without having to watch children and keep house may do wonders for a wife. One wife I greatly admire arranged with a friend to go on a river trip for a few days while her husband took care of their home and children.

Carried to an extreme, however, autonomy can destroy a marriage. It is well known that during prolonged separations "absence makes the heart grow fonder . . . for someone else." I am not encouraging prolonged or frequent separations, but an occasional time for *both* husband and wife to take a breather from their many responsibilities. Then, during this time, the partners may want to think about ways to be a better spouse and recommit themselves to their relationship upon returning.

It is unlikely that any two marriages have exactly the same degree of autonomy for husbands and wives. Different people have different expectations of autonomy. And the desire for autonomy may change within the marriage as the years pass. What is important is that each marriage partner examine his or her own need for autonomy and understand the autonomy expected by his or her spouse.

Four Phases of Marriage

The need for mutuality (joint identity and activities) and autonomy are part of the adjustments many people experience in marriage. Dr. Abraham Schmitt, marriage counselor and professor at the University of Pennsylvania, believes marriages that survive pass through four different phases of mutuality and autonomy as shown in the following chart (modified):

A Model for a Maturing Marriage
(Becoming "One")

In his article, "Conflict and Ecstasy: A Model for a Maturing Marriage,"[4] Professor Schmitt states that successful marriages go through the phases of Ecstasy I, Conflict, Ecstasy II, and Freedom.

Ecstasy I is the romantic part of mate selection. At the peak moment of closeness, two people commit themselves to marriage for life. This is a time experienced as intense union, when a couple's total needs for intimacy are met.

The Conflict phase begins soon after the marriage as the two people attempt to communicate their wants and needs to each other. They want each other to know that they are two different human beings whose identities are not to be lost in the relationship. During the conflict phase the couple begins to ascertain exactly what they will and will not derive from their marriage. And they begin to determine which of their needs will be met and which were just dreams. A mature couple can pass through the conflict phase without being smothered by the union or devastated by separation.

The third phase, Ecstasy II, begins when a couple realizes that both partners are unique individuals who make valuable contributions to the marriage. They begin to value rather than be threatened by their differences.

Ecstasy II is followed by the fourth and most rewarding phase—Freedom. In this phase, the partners feel free to be close and free to be separate as needed for psychological welfare.

Dr. Schmitt suggests that the couples in phase two, Conflict, should not give up, but should realize that the next phase, Ecstasy II, is attainable.

A loving marriage is not two organisms feeding on each other for sustenance; it is two separate beings, developing in different ways but at the same time touching each other's lives profoundly.

High Ego Strength

An important finding of a study by Ammons and Stinnet[5] was that the happily married couples they studied had high ego strength and could function apart from each other. A majority (seventy-five percent) of the respondents expressed a moderate need to make independent judgments and take independent actions. Only two percent expressed high dependency needs, and not one of the respondents reported high needs to accept undue blame or admit inferiority.

According to Ammons and Stinnet, the importance of healthy ego strength to a happy marriage appears relevant to forming rewarding personal relationships, handling stress well, and attaining sexual gratification. They also note that stress and conflict are inevitable in an intimate relationship. Stress can be debilitating for those with low ego strength. Their underlying insecurity and fear of losing the relationship may cause them to cling to their mate in neurotic desperation. High ego strength enables couples to weather stressful times and frees them to solve their problems while leaving each partner's integrity intact.

Acknowledging Individual Strengths

It is apparent that individual strengths are crucial to a satisfying marriage. But if you were asked to list your own personal strengths, could you do it? And could you identify those of your husband or wife? Some would be able to list one or two, but the vast majority would have a difficult time doing so. Why? In his book *More Joy in Your Marriage*,[6] Dr. Herbert Otto notes, "Our research in human potentialities indicates that fewer than 1 out of 110 persons ever take time to list the good qualities they have. When asked to enumerate both their weaknesses and strengths, most people will list approximately three times as many weaknesses as strengths."

Our preoccupation with our personal weaknesses can affect our marriage. According to Dr. Otto, what we think of ourselves has much to do with how we see and relate to others. If we see ourselves as lopsided, with more weaknesses than strengths, we are likely to be more conscious of another person's weaknesses than we are of his strengths.

To help a married couple become more aware of each other's strengths, Dr. Otto has devised an exercise called "His and Her Strengths."

You and your wife should take a piece of paper and at the top write "My Strengths." Then write down all the good things you perceive about yourselves. Write for five or ten minutes but do not show your list to your spouse yet.

On the other side of the paper write "My Spouse's Strengths" and write all the good traits that you see in your spouse. Write as much as you can in five or ten minutes.

After you have completed both lists, take turns reading your lists aloud. Add to your list any strengths mentioned by your spouse that are not already on your list.

Avoid discussing shortcomings or problems during this exercise. If one of you starts to mention a weakness, the other should remind him that only strengths are being discussed.

Dr. Otto concludes, "All of us rejoice when someone we care about recognizes our positive qualities or that we have done something well. It also makes us feel good if we can praise someone we love about specific strengths."

The "His and Her Strengths" exercise helps a couple increase their awareness of their strengths and correct each other's lopsided perceptions of their weaknesses.

Dimensions of Privacy

Wives, as well as husbands, need privacy on occasion. Contrary to popular belief, there is no one single type of privacy. At least that is the conclusion of Dr. Darhl Pedersen. In *Perceptual and Motor Skills*,[7] Dr. Pedersen reports that there are at least six types of privacy, which suggests that privacy may vary from time to time according to circumstances and the individual's need. In addition, people may also have a favorite kind of privacy. The six types of privacy identified by Dr. Pedersen are:

Intimacy with family. A person is alone with family members to maximize family relationships.

Intimacy with friends. A person is alone with friends to maximize interpersonal relationships.

Reserve. A person withholds comments about personal aspects of himself from others.

Anonymity. A person is surrounded by others but does not expect to be recognized.

Solitude. A person is alone in a private area such as a bedroom or study.

Isolation. A person is alone in a remote area.

According to this study, there are many ways a husband can help his wife find some privacy.

A husband may help his wife find *intimacy with family* simply by making time for the family to be alone without distractions or interruptions. This might be on a camping trip, on a hike, or during family devotionals.

A husband might encourage *intimacy with friends* by helping his wife to have an occasional night out. Not long ago Susan wanted to see a certain movie, and I didn't really want to go. I suggested she call a friend and invite her. Much to our surprise, the friend had to ask her husband if she could go, and he said, "No! Women aren't supposed to go anywhere without their husbands." We were quite shocked at his response and wondered if his attitude is typical of many husbands.

Privacy by *reserve* could be found by a husband not demanding that his wife reveal all of her thoughts and opinions. Sometimes what she thinks may be none of his business! Either too little or too much disclosure may hinder communication. There must be a balance between disclosure and reserve.

The need for *anonymity* might be met in several ways. Some people like to go to a ball game and become one of the several thousand in the crowd. I like to stroll through shopping malls and was surprised to find that Susan enjoys this too. Many people find anonymity by going to the beach or a public gathering where they are surrounded by people who don't know them. A movie star wearing sunglasses is a classic example of someone trying to maintain anonymity.

A husband can help his wife find *solitude* right in their own home by not invading her privacy in a study, sewing room, or bedroom. He can also keep curious children from intruding. Encouraging a wife to find solitude may be just what she needs to do it.

Isolation is difficult to find, but it can be done, especially in natural settings such as the mountains, the woods, the beach, or the desert. A husband might arrange to take over the household duties for a few days while his wife visits such a spot. One woman wrote to me about her retreat:

"Shall I tell you what I found? Silence. Beautiful and quiet. I was alone. I walked in the hills, I studied my scriptures, I knelt and prayed in the mountain trees, I watched sunsets and listened to the crickets and locusts at night. I heard no sounds but the words I spoke when I prayed as I walked along the fields. I slept and awoke in the mornings, and didn't have to get up. I would stay in bed and listen to the birds sing. I meditated, and found sunrises in hills. I basked in the most elegant three days of my life.

"At the end of that time I came home, refreshed, to begin again. And I could begin. And when I think of those days, I think of an oasis—of peace."

I began this chapter with a quotation from Kahlil Gibran. I close with another that expresses the need for balance in mutuality and autonomy in marriage:

But let there be spaces in your togetherness,
And let the winds of the heavens dance between you.
Love one another, but make not a bond of love:
Let it rather be a moving sea between the shores of
    your souls.
Fill each other's cup, but drink not from one cup.
Give each other of your bread but eat not from
    the same loaf.
Sing and dance together and be joyous,
    but let each one of you be alone.
Even as the strings of a lute are alone
    though they quiver with the same music.[8]

8

TIME

Many wives in my survey wished they had more time alone with their husbands. They wrote:

"I appreciate it when my husband takes time out to make me feel like a woman. I feel like a mother, a daughter, a daughter-in-law, a Church member, and so on all day long. I need to be reminded from time to time that I am a woman, a wife, and me. My husband has done this by leaving Friday as my day to do what I want. Usually we go out to dinner. It was easy to do B.C. [Before Children and Before (intense) Church activity], but it has become increasingly difficult. Now we go to weddings and other functions, but at least we are together. *Spending time together is an absolute necessity.*" (Italics added.)

"I appreciated it when my husband took a week off work (he works every day except Sunday) and took me, just me, on a vacation. He is a retail store manager and feels very responsible in his position. It made me feel very loved when he set his work aside for that long just to be with me."

While some husbands spend adequate time with their wives, many do not. One wife wrote, "I would like him to sense my moods and respond with some time especially for me when I am tired, frustrated, or burdened. I would like this time without him complaining and without having to ask for it."

Another young woman said, "In the future, I would appreciate more planning for time together. Specifically, setting aside time for just us. Time to share experiences, develop interests we can share, become better acquainted, and just be good friends."

An older woman wished her husband would just "offer to go out in the evening for a walk or bike ride."

Wives do expect an occasional night out with their husbands. One happy wife said, "I enjoy going on little trips with him or just a date to dinner or a show. But it doesn't have to cost anything to make me happy. All he has to do is let me know he's glad I'm there." And another satisfied housewife simply wrote, "We have a regular date night. He tries very hard to follow the advice of our church leaders, who say we should go out alone as husband and wife."

Some wives don't want to go out on the spur of the moment. One wife admonished husbands, "Plan ahead for dates. Spur of the moment planning is difficult, and by planning you can get more in. Or, it can just make you happier in looking forward to the time together."

Television

Many wives feel they often compete with the television set for the time their husbands spend at home. One wife observed, "Because my husband is usually married to the television, I was pleased and flattered that last Sunday he consented to go for a walk with me. We sat on the grass and talked and watched the sunset, and generally enjoyed each other's company. The personal attention that I rarely get was truly appreciated and fondly remembered."

Another wife noted, "As for something my husband could do in the future, I would appreciate more time spent together in

the evenings. He is a very busy man with heavy church responsibilities, and when he has an evening at home, he spends it doing paperwork and then watches television." Another young
woman was rather vehement about television: "Some night
after the kids are asleep, I wish he would, without my asking,
help me straighten up the house and then turn the television off
(I hate that television!). Then we could spend the evening
hours together."

The television even regulates what time husbands and
wives go to bed, sometimes separately. One disappointed wife
wrote, "Another expectation is less television. He could use
this time to talk to me. Why do we have to wait every night until after the news and weather report before going to bed?"

Some marriage counselors advise newlyweds not to become
highly involved with the television, particularly during their
first year of marriage. Television can subtly steal the time that
you should be devoting to your spouse and later to your children. It will take away the most wonderful hours of your day—
hours that could be spent communicating, sharing, and learning to relate to one another. There is no giving or receiving
when you spend your time watching television.

Sports and Hobbies

Often when wives are not competing with the television,
they become sport or hobby widows. A few years ago at Southern Illinois University, I taught a class for married couples. One
evening I asked them to anonymously list their major concerns
in their marriages.

Later I compiled a list of their responses and found that a
major problem was the husbands' involvement in sports. Many
of the husbands spent almost every weekend driving to Saint
Louis to watch the Cardinals during baseball and football
seasons. Most of the time the wives were left behind.

One wife recently wrote to me about the annual deer hunt,
"I wish he would give up deer hunting. It causes so many problems. As much as six weeks before and two weeks after he treats
me rudely. If I go with him and his family, he ignores me and

125

talks to them. If I say anything, he accuses me of being a stick-in-the-mud."

Not long ago I counseled a couple on the verge of divorce. Part of the wife's concern was her husband's excessive involvement with golf. I suggested they plan some joint activities during the following week. They agreed to try seven more days of marriage to see what might be done.

They agreed that on Monday they would go out dining, and on Wednesday, they would stay home and review some personal matters together. Then came Thursday.

On Thursday afternoon, she suggested they drive into a nearby city for a musical play. He replied, "No, I have a golf game that afternoon. I must be there." I reminded him that this might be their last week together. He said it didn't matter—the golf game had been planned for several weeks and he couldn't cancel it. His wife and I tried to help him see that his marriage was more important than the golf game, but somehow he couldn't see how his game interfered with his marriage. His wife became furious and told me there would be no need for further counseling. She walked out of the room. And her husband had the audacity to ask, "What's wrong with her?" Is it any wonder that they divorced just two weeks later?

Some husbands, however, are sensitive to their wives' concerns and take their wives along. One wife wrote, "When other fellows ask my husband to go jogging, he tells them, 'No thanks. I'd rather jog with my wife.' The other fellows would be more challenging for him because I am not really a fast jogger. But it makes me think he sincerely enjoys my company."

Many husbands claim they are too busy to spend time with their wives or families. But being too busy is not the real issue. Husbands somehow find time for the things they want to do.

Occupations

Wives often compete for time with their husbands' jobs. And many wives find they are, at best, a close second. In some instances, it isn't even close.

A few years ago, William H. Whyte wrote an article called

"The Wives of Management."[1] He asked some questions that few dare contemplate: Does a man derive his major satisfactions from his occupation or from his marriage? Where does a man spend most of his time?

Of course everyone knows that the answer to the first question should be that a man's major satisfactions in life come from his marriage and home.

However, while this belief is common, Whyte questions whether or not it is correct. He asks:

1. If his marriage and home are a man's Shangri-la, why is he so frequently absent? Whyte notes that husbands want to turn over more of the child-rearing responsibilities to their wives than the wives want to assume. One of the most frequent complaints of wives, according to Whyte, is summed up in one sentence: "He doesn't spend enough time with me or the children." And in most cases, husbands agree.

2. If a man's major interests are home and marriage, why is it, as many psychologists note, that men show a remarkable ability to repress home worries while on the job? Rarely, however, can men shut out occupational concerns while at home.

3. If a man's marriage and home life are more fulfilling than his occupation, why is the prospect of retirement so threatening? If marriage has precedence over job, retirement would seem to be something for which a couple could strive—time to be together.

4. If a husband had to make a choice, which would he take: an increasingly satisfying work life and a proportionately less satisfying home life—or the opposite? Whyte suggests that many would be surprised at the answer.

"Doing all this work for the family," Whyte notes, "is a rationalization for many men. Even if the money were not the incentive, many U.S. males would continue to knock themselves out while highly involved in some type of employment."

Granted that most men work to support their families, two additional questions must still be asked. First, where do employed husbands spend most (and often the best) of their waking hours? With their wives and families, or at work? Second, when husbands are not working, where or with whom

127

do they spend their time? With wife and family or in pursuit of other interests?

If wives are going to get the time they want from husbands, husbands may have to rearrange their priorities.

Psychological Absence

When husbands and wives are together, sometimes the husbands aren't "really" there. A few years ago, some family life specialists studied some fishermen and their families living on a European coast. They wanted to know how these men could go to sea for months at a time without disrupting their families.

One important thing the researchers learned was that the husbands were not gone by choice nor did they want to "get away" from their wives and children. Fishing was their only means of making a living, so periodically the men would have to be separated from their loved ones.

The researchers also found that even though the husbands were physically absent from the home during their fishing trips, they were psychologically present. The fishermen often thought about their wives and looked forward to returning home. The wives often talked to their children about the men and expressed concern for their safety, and all eagerly looked forward to being reunited.

While many men are physically present in the home, they are often psychologically absent. Too many husbands bring home unfinished work or spend a disproportionate amount of time working at hobbies, reading newspapers, taking catnaps, or watching television. A husband's physical presence in the home should be matched by his psychological presence. Wives don't like to be ignored, particularly when husbands are at home.

How Much Time?

Two years ago, I attended a convention where Dr. Stephen Glenn of the Family Development Institute in Washington, D. C., was the speaker. He reported that, on the average, a husband and wife in the United States spend approximately thirteen minutes a day talking to each other on a personal basis.

According to Dr. Glenn, mealtimes do not count because "conversations" such as "Please pass the butter" or "Is there any more casserole?" are less than personal. Most table-talk is nothing more than simultaneous monologues, and with children present, it is difficult to carry on a conversation about marriage.

Other occasions that don't count for time together include PTA meetings, social engagements, and even some church meetings. At such functions there is little time for personal interaction.

Going to movies and watching television don't count either unless you have acquired the knack of intimate conversation over popcorn or between commercials.

And time spent discussing daily routines of running the home or rearing the children doesn't count either. Wives simply expect time with their husbands alone.

9

HELP

When I was growing up, I heard a song written by Al Frisch about people in love. The first line was "Two different worlds, we live in two different worlds." That this is often true is indicated in the "Profile of a Loving Husband."

It is almost as if husbands don spacesuits and blast off each morning for another planet, the world of work. At the end of the day they reenter the home atmosphere for a few hours with their wives. However, husbands often see home as a place to refuel so they can go on exploring worlds away from home.

Wives usually assume three major responsibilities noted by Rainwater, Coleman, and Hanel in their article "Day In, Day Out"[1]: household management, child servicing, and husband servicing.

But if wives nurture their children and to some degree their husbands, who nurtures the wives? How long can they give without, in turn, receiving? Wives want and need nurturing from husbands. And one way husbands can nurture their wives is to become involved in her world and help with her many responsibilities.

Wives Expect Help

That wives would, on occasion, appreciate their husbands helping them is shown by the following comments:

"When my husband gives me his time and helps me, I appreciate him the most. I have decided that I must feel this way because of the many hours I spend every day and week giving personal service to him and our children. Recently he gave extra help when I was chairman of the PTA carnival, president of Primary, and teaching in that organization when no teachers were available. This meant my husband had to rearrange his work schedule since I was so busy during the week. Help with housework or the children, especially when they are small, is what I appreciate most."

"I think the thing I would appreciate most is to have my husband's help on special occasions. When he knows I have to get ready to go somewhere, I would like him to come home a little earlier and help with supper or the children or even just be there so getting ready will not be such a hectic experience for me. Usually by the time I get everything ready so I can go somewhere, I'm too tired and discouraged even to want to go."

"My husband shows his love to me the most when he helps with the household tasks and doesn't criticize when something isn't done. Many men insist that they shouldn't be involved with the work at home because they 'work all day' and are tired when they get home. Well, that is a cheap cop-out. I also work outside the home as a nurse and know what it feels like to come home tired. I believe that neither the man's nor the woman's responsibility to each other stops with a paycheck."

Do Husbands Really Help?

One of the biggest shocks of my marriage occurred one summer when Susan wanted to take a few classes at the university. I was not teaching for a few months and planned to do some writing. So, being the big-hearted husband that I am (or thought I was!), I agreed to become a house-husband and take over her responsibilities while she went back to school. No big problem, I thought, I'll just fix a few meals now and then and make sure the baby sleeps all day, and I will be able to write magnificent articles. Little did I know.

That summer turned out to be a transition in our marriage. Not that I became Super Helper, but I did become keenly aware and more appreciative of what Susan and other wives do to rear children and manage a home. And I would like to think that I now help more than I did before.

Before that, I had agreed to take out the garbage most of the time (which was fifty-one percent to me and ninety-nine percent to her) and do some of the major lifting and more strenuous work around the yard. Beyond that, I did little else. And what I didn't know was that I was typical of most husbands in the United States.

In the July 1981 issue of *Family Therapy News*[2] is a fascinating article by Nadine Brozman, "Men and Housework: Do They or Don't They?" Her conclusion? They don't, regardless of all the reports to the contrary. Nadine Brozman summarized the findings of four major advertising agencies that were interested in knowing if they should focus some of their advertising on husbands who might be purchasing major household items and working in the home. They found that "the American husband may say he helps out at home, but save for tending the lawn and taking out the garbage, he's not contributing much."

Much of the research focused on husbands who assist working wives. A report by Batten, Barten, Durstine, and Osborne Advertising Agency concluded, "Today's man wants his woman to work at two jobs—one outside the home and one inside the home. Men may be sympathetic to the fact that this is a tough juggling act for any woman. Yet the majority are not willing to lift the traditional household responsibilities from their wives. The indications are that men would rather pay for labor-saving devices for their wives than labor at wifely tasks themselves."

Most of the men in this study said they expected a wife to assume major responsibility for household chores, whether she was working outside the home or not. More than seventy-five percent said their wives were primarily responsible for cooking, and seventy-eight percent considered cleaning the bathroom their wives' domain. The chore that men seemed most unlikely to do was the laundry.

According to Barbara Michael, vice president of Doyle Dane Bernbach Advertising Agency, "The major disadvantage that the typical husband perceives in having a working wife is the effect not upon the children but upon himself; a husband has to spend more time on household chores that he doesn't like. And with the exception of lawns and home repairs, he pretty much doesn't like any of them. The fear of detrimental effects on children was followed in depth of concern by fear of a decline in cleanliness standards and a sense that the extra income was not sufficient compensation for inconvenience."

A study by Cunningham and Walsh Advertising Agency showed that if husbands do help, it is mostly in grocery shopping and some cooking. They reported, "When not cooking, some husbands are helping around the house in other ways. Taking out the garbage is the man's primary household assignment. Almost half vacuum most or some of the time and two out of five wash the dishes. One in three makes beds and loads the washing machine, while one in four cleans the bathrooms, dusts, and dries dishes. Husbands leave the cleaning of the refrigerator and oven to their mates."

This study shows that a sizeable *minority* of husbands are taking more responsibility around the house. For the majority, the apron strings have not yet been tied behind their backs.

Still, the prediction is made that what is now a small nucleus of homemaking husbands will grow to a significant segment of society in the future. One such favorable study by Benton and Bowles Advertising Agency of 452 married men indicated that eighty-eight percent agreed that a husband should at least "help out" with chores, particularly if his wife is employed. In a two-week period, eighty percent of the husbands with children under twelve years of age had taken care of the children. And forty-seven percent had helped cook a meal; thirty-nine percent had vacuumed the house; thirty-three percent had cooked an entire meal; thirty-two percent had done the food shopping; and twenty-nine percent had done the laundry.

Perhaps husbands will assist their wives more with household tasks in the future, and not only because it would be a nice thing to do; simply put, wives expect it!

Wives and Stress

If your marriage is like most, you probably have your ups and downs. But think for a moment. What was happening the last time your wife hit the "down" side of life? Was there a death of a close friend or family member? Were there troubles with in-laws? Was a child about to leave home? If you could think of specific events that produced stress, you validated the findings of Dr. Thomas H. Holmes and Dr. Richard H. Rahe of the University of Washington School of Medicine. Their study suggests there are particular times when husbands need to be particularly attentive and offer a helping hand.

Writing in the *Journal of Psychosomatic Research*,[3] Holmes and Rahe described a way to correlate stressful events with sickness. They predicted a relationship between stress and illness, and tested their hypothesis with more than five thousand patients.

The two doctors devised their Schedule of Recent Experiences, which assigns numerical values to typical events in people's lives. These events include marriage, death in the family, changes in a job, pregnancy, a large mortgage, and so on. To use the Schedule, check off events that have happened to you within the last year.

Event	Value	Event	Value
Death of a close family member	63	Outstanding personal achievement	29
Personal injury or illness	53	Spouse begins or stops work	26
Fired from work	47	Starting or finishing school	26
Retirement	45	Change in living conditions	25
Change in family member's health	44	Revision of personal habits	24
		Trouble with boss	23
Pregnancy	40	Change in work hours, conditions	20
Sex difficulties	39		

134

Addition to family	39	Change in residence	20
Business readjustment	39	Change in schools	20
Change in financial status	38	Change in recreational habits	19
Death of close friend	37	Change in church activities	19
Change to different line of work	36	Change in social activities	18
		Mortgage or loan under $10,000	17
Change in number of marital arguments	35	Change in sleeping habits	16
Mortgage or loan over $10,000	31	Change in number of family	15
		Change in eating habits	15
Foreclosure of mortgage or loan	30	Vacation	13
		Christmas season	12
Son or daughter leaving home	29		
Trouble with in-laws	29		

Now add up the assigned values of these events. Holmes and Rahe found that a score of 150 would make one's chances of developing an illness or a health change about fifty percent. If your score is over 300 points, your chances of a health change are up to almost ninety percent. As the score increases, the probability that a health change will be a serious illness increases.

Many of the stressful events are ones that we generally consider to be occasions of joy and celebration. For instance, outstanding personal achievement has a value of 29, a vacation 13 (Susan and I recently had one that must have rated 63), and Christmas, "The Season to Be Jolly," 12. Positive events can produce stress as well as negative events.

Common events such as pregnancy (40), starting or finishing school (26), change in residence (20), change in sleeping habits (16), and change in eating habits (15) are particularly harmful only when they occur in clusters.

From the Holmes and Rahe study, it is evident we can have not only a bad day, but a bad year as well. And during such times husbands should be a little more patient, considerate, and helpful than usual.

Mutual Help

The importance of helping each other in marriage was demonstrated by a study in Great Britain a few years ago. Several people who had met in mental institutions later married each other, and the question arose, "Is marriage a viable relationship for the mentally impaired?"

In her book *Marriage and Mental Handicap*,[4] Janet Mattinson reported locating and interviewing thirty-six mentally handicapped couples who had been married from one to fifteen years.

She found that thirty-two of the thirty-six (eighty-nine percent) were still married. This is an impressive statistic when compared to the sixty percent of "normal" couples who stay together in the United States. How could mentally handicapped couples have a lower divorce rate? The answer was simple —they had learned to help each other.

In conjunction with the Department of Sociology in the University of Exeter, Mattinson interviewed the thirty-two couples still together. The following were among her findings:

1. Apparently the couples were able to quickly recognize their need of each other. They also recognized their own and each other's intellectual and other limitations and learned to help when needed.

2. The couples reported receiving a tremendous amount of satisfaction from helping each other.

3. The couples depended on each other in many areas of their married life. Working together, they were able to accomplish much more than they would have alone. While this is true in many marriages, it seemed to be a particularly striking characteristic of this group of mentally impaired people.

In summary, Janet Mattinson observed:

> I was particularly impressed by the mutual help these husbands and wives gave to each other and by the complementary nature of the partnerships. Recognizing their own intellectual and emotional limitations, they used their partner for what they could not do. . . . The success of many of these marriages seemed to be related to the initial expectation not having been too high. That they had done so much better than most people had expected them to do gave them enormous satisfaction. And some failure was not distressful to

them as it might have been to other people whose aims were higher. (P. 201.)

After reading this study, I really wonder who is normal. Who actually provides the best models for marriage? Who gives the help? Certainly we who deem ourselves to be at least average in intelligence have something to learn from these British couples. Perhaps we should admit that we all have limitations and learn to help each other. We could also lower our expectations of what our marriage partner should be, particularly if these expectations are unrealistic. And we could probably be more cooperative and thereby compensate for some of our weaknesses.

A Wife's Plimsoll Mark

Even though many wives undertake tremendous responsibilities, they have limits. And husbands have a particular responsibility to help when these limits are exceeded. These limits have been called by some the Plimsoll mark of mental health.

Samuel Plimsoll was born in Bristol, England, in 1824, and as a youth became interested in commercial shipping. He watched ships load and unload their cargos day after day. Young Samuel Plimsoll soon made a simple observation; regardless of the cargo space available, each ship had its maximum capacity. And after each ship exceeded its limit, it became likely to sink as it went to sea. Many did.

In 1868 Plimsoll entered Parliament for Derby and eight years later passed the Merchant Shipping Act, which prevented ships from sailing in unsafe conditions. One provision of Plimsoll's Act called for making calculations of how much each ship could carry. Marks or lines were then drawn on the hull of each ship, and as the ship was loaded with cargo, it would sink lower and lower into the water. Finally the water level on the side of the ship would reach the mark, and the ship was then loaded to capacity. These marks became known as Plimsoll marks.

Like ships, people have differing capacities to withstand

137

stress. Some stresses are unavoidable, but some we bring on ourselves. Many of these could be eliminated or reduced with a little foresight and effort. Examples of these avoidable stresses are excessive debt, frequent arguments, sexual difficulties, frequent changes in residence, unnecessary or elaborate remodeling and decorating, an increase or decrease in church activity, changes in eating habits or prolonged dieting, excessive weight gain, or an inordinate amount of time spent with sports or hobbies.

Every wife must establish her own Plimsoll line of what she can and cannot handle. Once the line is determined, a husband should help her monitor the load level and assist when the limit is being approached. As with ships, action must be taken when the level is exceeded.

There are at least three things a husband can do when his wife is overloaded. First, he can unload part of the cargo pound by pound or, depending on the condition of his wife, remove large portions immediately. Second, he can help redistribute the load. Sometimes ships and marriages become imbalanced because the load is not properly distributed. A husband may have to assume more of the responsibilities his wife has been carrying. Third, a husband may help his wife re-evaluate what must be carried now and what could be put off until another time. Wives might use the same three principles to help overburdened husbands.

Slave or Servant?

One important aspect of marital love is altruism, the practice of unselfish concern for the welfare of another. After discussing this concept in class not long ago, a student told me of a decision he and his wife made shortly after their marriage that had contributed to many years of fulfillment. They decided to be servants to each other, but never slaves.

The student said that a slave does something for someone else with little or no appreciation, and the services performed are expected rather than anticipated. But a servant, he said, does something for someone else because he wants to, and he gets satisfaction from helping another person.

Marriage might be more satisfying if we were more altruistic. Husbands should stop demanding service from their wives and start giving more appreciation and praise.

One Husband Who Helps

If any husband doubts whether or not his wife would appreciate some help around the house, he ought to consider the following letter I received from a wife not long ago:

Dear Dr. Barlow:

Your column in the *Deseret News* has inspired me to come straight to my typewriter and tell you about my husband, Phil.

Phil and I were married one year ago last Monday. We are both in our mid-thirties. We have both been previously married. We both have two children from our previous marriages, although his children live in Denver with their mother. My children live with us.

We were engaged for five months, to which I attribute the success of our marriage in a large part. We both have parallel ideals and goals. We are both totally committed to a successful marriage.

I was most impressed with my husband's love for me immediately after our marriage. He took another man's children into his home and into his heart and loved them without discrimination.

How does this show his love for me? I remember as a child hearing my mother say, "When someone does something nice for my children, they do something nice for me." I felt much the same way. Before our marriage, Phil learned how important it was to me to have him treat my children well. It all began with his honest effort to please me. It now has evolved into a genuine love and interest in "our" kids that comes from his love for his family.

From the beginning he has helped me by sharing in our household responsibilities. He cooks, cleans, and supervises the children. He can do the laundry as well as I can. He has never come home from work and planted himself in front of the television. When I'm free, he's free. When I'm working, he's working. All this in spite of the fact that I quit my job in December and have since been a full-time homemaker.

We are now expecting a much-wanted addition in March and I have been in bed with complications. My dear Phil comes home from work and plunges himself into dinner. He frequently serves me a beautiful meal in bed, feeds the kids, does the dishes, throws in a batch of laundry, plays UNO with the kids and me, gets the kids washed and ready for bed—all this and more with never a complaint.

What could he do in the future to show his love? Nothing more nor less than he has already done in the past. He is an unusual man, a patient and tireless husband. Even in trial there is always optimism in his voice.

I have no doubt that this will continue if I do my part. I love him, support him, believe in him, encourage him, praise him. In return, he gives it all back to me, twofold. Thank you for giving me a forum to openly adore my wonderful husband.

10

FINAL COMMENTS

Toward the end of his life Sigmund Freud wrote, "The great question . . . which I have not been able to answer, despite my thirty years of research into the feminine soul, is 'What does a woman want?' " (Quoted in Charles Rolo, *Psychiatry in American Life*, 1963.) You now have an advantage in that you know what many, in fact several hundred, wives expect from husbands. The most important expectations, however, are the ones each man's wife has of him, and it is important that she make these known.

Lloyd Ogilvie, in his article "Marriage As It Was Meant to Be,"[1] notes, "It is absolutely essential to clarify what two people need and expect in their marriage. . . . Most frustrations in marriage come from unexpressed desires and uncommunicated dreams. When these are brought out in the open, a new realizable agreement can be worked out. This needs to be done repeatedly and often."

Many husbands and wives become offended at lists of what the perfect husband or wife should be. I am among those who resist the "Paul and Patti Perfect" syndrome. A few months ago I was interviewed on a television call-in program about the "Profile of a Loving Husband." The interviewer introduced me as the professor who had a list of what the perfect husband should be. Because of his introduction, a few irate husbands called in asking how anyone could compile such a list. I explained that it was not my intention to compile such a list, nor, incidently, is that the purpose of this book. I have simply compiled some of the expectations wives have of their husbands and tried to indicate which of these are most important.

It is important that husbands know what other wives expect as well as knowing the expectations of their own wives. In a counseling session, a woman tried to explain to her husband that she liked him to touch her and hold her without always heading straight to bed for sexual relationships. After she told him, he became offended and said, "Oh, that's just you. You're the only woman in the world that feels that way!" At this point, I told him about the "Profile of a Loving Husband" and explained that the item "He expresses affection by touch without always having sexual relationships is a common expectation of many women. And his wife was elated to find that she was not alone in her expectation.

Husbands who read this book may also find that some of their wive's expectations are very similar to those of others. They cannot, therefore, dismiss them as idiosyncracies of their wives only.

A Word About Divorce

While I was training to be a marriage counselor at Florida State University, one of my professors asked an intriguing question: "Is divorce the enemy or ally of marriage?"

Some students recalled the heartaches and pain that divorce frequently brings and suggested it would be best for society if there were no divorces.

"What if," the professor continued, "there were no divorces? Once married there would be absolutely no way to get out of it no matter what." Carried to that extreme, we began to reconsider our opinions.

As long as people have the right to choose their marriage partners, unwise choices will sometimes be made. And even if an adequate choice is made, situations sometimes arise that make marriage difficult and in some cases impossible.

FINAL COMMENTS

I believe that no one should remain in a relationship where his or her life is threatened or sought. No marriage is worth a human life.

In addition, I believe no one need stay in a marriage where he or she is beaten or physically abused. Common sense dictates that no relationship gives men or women the right to strike each other.

In my opinion, there are also legitimate cases of mental cruelty where one or both marriage partners are emotionally abused over an extended period of time. Such cases are difficult to ascertain, but they often cause as much or more pain as physical abuse.

Certainly there are other circumstances that warrant divorce, including continued non-support or repeated infidelity. But in many marriages where husbands and wives are unhappy, divorce is only one option.

I agree with Roberta Temes, psychotherapist and assistant professor of psychiatry at Downstate Medical School in New York City. In a recent edition of *Psychology Today*[2] she wrote,

> Couples often consult me about a marriage that is no longer satisfying. They seek 'divorce counseling.' I tell them that divorce is only one option. Patience is a choice, too.
>
> I further tell such couples that there is pain in being single, in being married, and in being alive. Marriage does, however, provide a person to blame for pain. I must convince them that divorce is not a necessary ritual, that individuation and maturity can be achieved without shedding a spouse.
>
> Marriage needs new rules. My wish for my patients is that the solution of the 70's, which was to find a new mate when the current one was no longer need-fulfilling, will be obsolete. I hope the 80's solution will be to explore the absurdity of marital myths and develop rules to allow occasional unhappiness in marriage.

Dr. Temes's thoughts are noteworthy. All too often we demand of marriage what we seldom demand of any other aspect of life—perfection. As students, few of us constantly achieved 100-percent on all of our assignments. No adult always expects a 100 percent return on an investment. No cook is able to make a perfect cake 100 percent of the time, no matter how experienced. And a baseball player who gets a hit only thirty-three percent of the time is pretty well satisfied. Why, then, should we always expect perfection in marriage?

President Spencer W. Kimball said, "Divorce is not a cure for difficulty, but is merely an escape, and a weak one. We have come to realize also that the mere performance of a ceremony does not bring happiness and a successful marriage. Happiness does not come by pressing a button, as does the electric light; happiness is a state of mind and comes from within. It must be earned. It cannot be purchased with money; it cannot be taken for nothing."[3]

Marriage—an Act of Creation

A few weeks ago, I gave a talk on marriage to a group of newlyweds. After my talk a former student came up to see me. She and her husband, she said, had been happily married for three years. And it had been about that long since she had been in my class.

Like most teachers, I was curious about what she had learned in my class, so I asked her what from the class had most helped her marriage. She said the most important thing I ever taught her was that newlyweds should plant something together and watch it grow. As we discussed this concept, I realized that I had taught her something very important.

Suppose that as a couple you had a great ambition to have a beautiful garden, a place of peace and serenity with tall trees, shrubs, lawns, and flowers. What if you had the plot of ground and tools and then took your lawn chairs and sat down on your land and waited for your garden. How long would you have to wait? Waiting alone would not bring it about. You would have to learn all about soil chemistry, plants, and landscaping. You would have to work hard for months or even years. But one day your dream would come true, and you would be able to enjoy your beautiful garden.

So it is with marriage. Just because we say "I do" at a
ceremony, we expect a marriage to happen in some miraculous
way, not realizing that it takes time, hard work, and learning
new skills to have a satisfying marriage. This idea was beauti-
fully expressed in a poem years ago by an Englishwoman, Jan
Struther, who described marriage as an act of creation. She
wrote:

The raw materials of love are yours . . .
Fond hearts, and lusty blood, and minds in tune:
And so, dear innocents, you think yourselves
Lovers full-blown.

Am I, because I own
Chisel, mallet and stone,
A sculptor? And must he
Who hears a skylark and can hold a pen
A poet be?
If neither's so, why then
You're not yet lovers. But in time to come
(If senses grow not dulled nor spirit dumb)
By constant exercise of skill and wit,
By patient toil and judgement exquisite
Of body, mind and heart,
You may, my innocents, fashion
This tenderness, this liking, and this passion
Into a work of art.[4]

Appendix A

UNDERSTANDING YOUR EXPECTATIONS

While no husband can do all of the things below equally well at the same time, he can and perhaps should do some.

As a wife, review these items and then rank in order the *ten* characteristics most important to you in your marriage. For instance, if number fifteen is the most important, rank it first. If number five is second most important, rank it second. Continue until you have indicated *ten* characteristics you value in a loving husband.

Rank Order

_____ 1. He has concern and interest in my day and activities.

_____ 2. He gives genuine help around the house without being asked and without complaining.

_____ 3. He arranges time for me to relax and be alone.

_____ 4. He helps me attain sexual satisfaction in our relationship.

_____ 5. He brings me unexpected gifts, flowers or cards and sometimes writes a note attached to the gift.

_____ 6. He periodically fixes dinner or dines out with me to give me a break from domestic routines.

_____ 7. He expresses affection by touch without sexual overtones.

_____ 8. He often spends time alone with me without interruptions or distractions.

_____ 9. He puts away his own things without expecting me to pick up after him.

_____ 10. He communicates effectively with me by both talking and listening.

_____ 11. He comes home at the time indicated or notifies me well in advance.

_____ 12. He completes tasks he starts or agrees to do.

_____ 13. He expresses his love both by word and action.

_____ 14. He shows the same kind of personal interest in me as when we were dating.

_____ 15. He is concerned about my changing intellectual, emotional, social, and physical needs.

_____ 16. He understands how new clothes and physical appearance affect my self-esteem.

_____ 17. He encourages rather than discourages my individual endeavors.

_____ 18. He helps me attain my spiritual needs.

_____ 19. He takes an active part in rearing and disciplining our children.

_____ 20. He frequently compliments me.

After you have completed this exercise, you may want to share your results with your husband. You may also want to compare your results with the "Profile of a Loving Husband" (Appendix B).

Appendix B

PROFILE
OF A LOVING HUSBAND
(*Deseret News* Survey)

Rank Order   *Item*
1. He communicates effectively with me by both talking and listening.
2. He expresses his love both by word and action.
3. He expresses affection by touch without sexual overtones.
4. He takes an active part in rearing and disciplining our children.
5. He helps me attain my spiritual needs.
6. He is concerned about my changing intellectual, emotional, social, and physical needs.
7. He encourages rather than discourages my individual endeavors.
8. He often spends time alone with me without interruptions or distractions.
9. He gives genuine help around the house without being asked and without complaining.
10. He helps me attain sexual satisfaction in our relationship.

Appendix C

MEASURING YOUR MARRIAGE POTENTIAL

A simple test "Measuring Your Marriage Potential"[1] has been constructed by David and Vera Mace from Winston-Salem, North Carolina.

The Maces view marriage not as an unchanging relationship, but as a fluid, flexible interaction because goals in marriage constantly change. The Maces use the term "marital growth" to describe this process.

This test is self-administered and self-scored. All that is needed is a pen or pencil and a piece of paper. It can be taken without any advance preparation. A husband and wife should take it separately and then compare their scores and discuss the implications. Here is the test:

Listed below are ten areas of a marital relationship:
1. Common goals and values
2. Commitment to growth
3. Communication skills
4. Creative use of conflict
5. Appreciation and affection
6. Agreement on male/female roles
7. Cooperation and teamwork
8. Sexual fulfillment
9. Money management
10. Parent effectiveness

Each partner should write down the ten areas and enter a score, on a scale of zero to ten, to the right of each item. First go through the list and make a quick response. Then take a little more time to go over the areas and revise the scores if you think it is necessary. *The score represents where the marriage now stands in relation to where it could be if every possible resource were put to work in bringing it up to its full potential.*

A perfect score of ten, for example, for "Appreciation and Affection" would mean that neither partner ever missed an opportunity to give warm support and praise. A score of zero, on the other hand, would suggest that every opportunity is passed by. Relatively few couples, according to the Maces, rate their marriage at either extreme of zero or ten. Most scores fall somewhere in-between.

After each person has evaluated the ten categories, the scores should be added up. The resulting figure represents a percentage of the marriage potential that person has assigned to the relationship. The difference between the assigned score and 100 indicates the marriage potential yet unattained.

The next step is critical. The Maces suggest that the couple set a time when they can be alone together, uninterrupted, for at least an hour. During this period they should compare scores for the separate areas and the total score.

Nearly all couples who have taken this test, according to the Maces, have found it to be a significant experience. Many find their scores nearly identical, which suggests that their separate perceptions of the marriage as a whole are similar. When a significant disparity in a score exists, it suggests that a closer examination should be made of that area. The couple should discuss why they placed such different values on this particular part of their marriage.

If the scores are identical or very close, and low, clearly some work should be done. The Maces counsel such couples not to be discouraged about these low scores because "they mean you have money in the bank that you've never used. There are some good things waiting to be claimed."

For many couples, the discussion of the test is very challenging. It means facing some of the realities in their marriage

150

they may have previously avoided. Often the partners know but have never jointly faced the reality that specific areas of their marriage can be improved.

After discussing their scores, the couple should plan steps that both agree upon to improve their relationship in their deficient areas. They could write down and sign their plan so that they have a written commitment to which they can refer.

The Maces warn against the danger of attempting to change too much too quickly. "Do it in easy, manageable steps," they caution. "If you try to jump over a four-foot wall together and you're only able to clear a three-foot wall, you're both going to hurt yourselves." They further suggest that the couple share their commitment with another couple or couples to whom they can report progress, or with a counselor.

A final interesting aspect of this test is that it can be repeated. Since the measure of marriage potential used is subjective, the scores can change over time. As you gain clearer understanding of yourselves and each other, you may alter your evaluation of what is possible for your marriage. Your scores will change as you move toward a more realistic perception of what you are capable of achieving together.

You may want to change the list of areas to be evaluated. If you do not have children, for instance, you may want to drop parent effectiveness and add another area such as decision making, use of time together, balancing separateness and togetherness, or spiritual development.

NOTES

Preface

[1]Spencer W. Kimball, *Priesthood*, Salt Lake City: Deseret Book Company, 1981, pp. 4-5.

[2]Sidney M. Jourard, "Reinventing Marriage, The Perspective of a Psychologist," in *The Family in Search of a Future*, edited by Herbert A. Otto, New York: Appleton-Century Crofts, 1970, pp. 43-44.

Chapter 1

[1]*The Family Touch*, Atlanta: International Family Association, May 1980.

[2]Millard Bienvenu, "Measure of Marital Communication," *The Family Coordinator*, vol. 19, 1970, pp. 26-31.

[3]Paul Hauck and Edmund Kean, *Marriage and the Memo Method*, Philadelphia: Westminister, 1975.

[4]Larry Hof and William Miller, *Marriage Enrichment: Philosophy, Process, and Program*, Bowie, Maryland: Brady, 1981.

[5]Albert Ellis and Robert Harper, *A Guide to Successful Marriage*, Hollywood, California: Wilshire, 1972.

[6]David and Vera Mace, *How to Have a Happy Marriage*, Nashville: Abingdon, 1977.

[7]Walter McGraw, "Plants Are Only Human," *Argosy*, vol. 368, no. 6, June 1969, p. 23.

[8]Paul Schauble and Clara Hill, "A Laboratory Approach to Treatment in Marriage Counseling: Training in Communication Skills," *The Family Coordinator*, vol. 25, 1976, pp. 277-84.

[9]Robert Wilke, *Tell Me Again, I'm Listening*, Nashville: Abingdon, 1973, pp. 25-39.

Chapter 2

[1]Quoted by J. Richard Udry in *The Social Context of Marriage*, New York: J.B. Lippincott Co., 1974, p. 133.

[2]Carlfred B. Broderick, *Marriage and the Family*, New Jersey: Prentice-Hall, 1979, pp. 187-94.

[3]*Ibid.*, p. 194.

[4]James Dobson, *What Wives Wish Their Husbands Knew About Women*, Wheaton, Illinois: Tyndale House Publishers, 1975.

[5]William George Jordan, "Little Problems of Married Life," *Improvement Era*, Salt Lake City: The Church of Jesus Christ of Latter-day Saints, July 1911.

[6]W. Robert Beavers, "Lessons From a Dancing Chicken," *Family Therapy News*, Newspaper of the American Association of Marriage and Family Therapy, vol. 12, no. 3, May 1981.

Chapter 3

[1]Ed Wheat, *Love-Life*, Grand Rapids, Michigan: Zondervan, 1980.

[2]Paul Ammons and Nick Stinnet, "The Vital Marriage: A Closer Look," *Family Relations*, vol. 29, 1980, pp. 37-42.

[3]Carol Tavis and Susan Sadd, *The Redbook Report on Female Sexuality*, New York: Delacorte, 1977.

[4]*Writings of Parley P. Pratt*, edited and published by Parker Pratt Robinson, Salt Lake City, 1952, pp. 52-54.

[5]Hugh B. Brown, *You and Your Marriage*, Salt Lake City: Bookcraft, 1960.

[6]Jessie Bernard, *The Future of Marriage*, New York: World, 1972.

[7]J. Richard Udry, *The Social Context of Marriage*, New York: J. B. Lippincott Company, 1974.

[8]Lloyd Saxton, *The Individual, Marriage, and the Family*, 3rd ed., Belmont, California: Wadsworth Publishing Company, 1977.

[9]Henry Bowman and Graham Spanier, *Modern Marriage*, New York: McGraw Hill, 1977.

[10]Carlfred Broderick, *Couples: How to Confront Problems and Maintain Loving Relationships*, New York: Simon and Schuster, 1979.

[11]Isadore Rubin, *Sexual Life After Sixty*, New York: New American Library, 1965, pp. 42-52.

Chapter 4

[1]David Knox, *Marriage Happiness*, Champaign, Illinois: Research Press Co., 1971.

[2]Larry Hof and William Miller, *Marriage Enrichment: Philosophy, Process, and Program*, Bowie, Maryland: Brady, 1981.

[3]Rudolf Dreikurs, *Children: The Challenge*, New York: Hawthorn Books, Inc., 1964.

[4]E. E. LeMasters, *Parents in Modern America*, Homewood, Illinois: Dorsey Press, 1970.

[5]Rudolf Dreikurs, *Social Equality: The Challenge of Today*, Chicago: Henry Regnery Co., 1971.

[6]Dreikurs, *Children: The Challenge*.

[7]Kahlil Gibran, *The Prophet*, New York: Alfred A. Knopf, 1960, pp. 17-18.

Chapter 5

[1]Spencer W. Kimball, *Marriage*, Salt Lake City: Deseret Book Co., 1978, pp. 39-41.

[2]Eda LeShan, *The Wonderful Crisis of Middle Age*, New York: David McKay Co. Inc., 1973.

Chapter 6

[1]Margaret E. Sangster, "Our Own," in *Best-Loved Poems of*

the American People, New York: Garden City Books, 1936, p. 59.

[2]Nick Stinnet and James Walters, *Relationships in Marriage and Family*, New York: Macmillan Publishing Co., 1977.

[3]Spencer W. Kimball, *Marriage*, Salt Lake City: Deseret Book Company, 1978, pp. 46-47.

[4]Neal A. Maxwell, *The Smallest Part*, Salt Lake City: Deseret Book Company, 1973, p. 59.

[5]James Dobson, *What Wives Wish Their Husbands Knew About Women*, Wheaton, Illinois: Tyndale House Publishers, 1975.

[6]Carlfred Broderick, *Marriage and the Family*, New Jersey: Prentice-Hall, 1979, pp. 187-94.

[7]Robert O. Blood, *Marriage*, 2nd ed., New York: The Free Press, 1969.

[8]Lee Headley, *People Around You Can Make You Fat*, New York: Popular Library, 1979.

[9]Gerald Smith and Alice Phillips, *Me and You and Us*, New York: Peter H. Wyden, Inc., 1971, p. 89.

Chapter 7

[1]Kahlil Gibran, *The Prophet*, New York: Alfred A. Knopf, 1960, p. 16.

[2]Lloyd Saxton, *The Individual, Marriage, and the Family*, 3rd ed., Belmont, California: Wadsworth Publishing Company, 1977.

[3]Robert O. Blood, *Marriage*, 2nd ed., New York: The Free Press, 1969, p. 292.

[4]Abraham and Dorothy Schmitt, "Conflict and Ecstasy: A Model for a Maturing Marriage," in *Marriage and Family Enrichment: New Perspectives and Programs*, edited by Herbert A. Otto, Nashville: Abingdon, 1976, pp. 110-20.

[5]Paul Ammons and Nick Stinnet, "The Vital Marriage: A Closer Look," *Family Relations*, vol. 29, 1980, pp. 37-42.

[6]Herbert A. Otto, *More Joy in Your Marriage*, New York: Hawthorn Books Inc., 1969, pp. 75-79.

[7]Darhl M. Pedersen, "Dimensions of Privacy," *Perceptual and Motor Skills*, vol. 48, 1979, pp. 1291-97.

[8]Kahlil Gibran, *The Prophet*, New York: Alfred A. Knopf, 1960, pp. 15-16.

Chapter 8

[1]William Whyte, "The Wives of Management," in *Reflections on Marriage*, edited by William N. Stephens, New York: Thomas Y. Crowell Co. Inc., 1968, pp. 271-91.

Chapter 9

[1]Lee Rainwater, Richard Coleman, and Gerald Handel, "Day In, Day Out," in *Reflections on Marriage*, edited by William N. Stephens, New York: Thomas Y. Crowell Co., 1968, pp. 251-70.

[2]Nadine Brozman, "Men and Housework: Do They or Don't They?" *Family Therapy News*, Newspaper of the American Association for Marriage and Family Therapy, vol. 12, no. 4, July 1981.

[3]Thomas Holmes and Richard Rahe, "The Social Readjustment Rating Scale," *Journal of Psychosomatic Research*, vol. 11, 1967, pp. 213-18.

[4]Janet Mattison, *Marriage and Mental Handicap: A Study of Subnormality in Marriage*, Pittsburgh, Pennsylvania: University of Pittsburgh Press, 1971.

Chapter 10

[1]Lloyd Ogilvie, "Marriage As It Was Meant to Be," in *Making More of Your Marriage*, edited by Gary R. Collins, Waco, Texas: Word Books, Publishers, 1976, pp. 21-22.

[2]*Psychology Today*, May 1981, p. 17.

[3]Spencer W. Kimball, *Marriage*, Salt Lake City: Deseret Book Company, 1978, p. 35.

[4]Jan Struther, "Epithalamium," reprinted by permission of Curtis Brown, Ltd., London, on behalf of the estate of Jan Struther.

Appendix C

[1]*Family Coordinator*, January 1978, pp. 63-67. Also in *Readers Digest*, July 1980, pp. 63-68.

INDEX